A Catholic Case Against

SEGREGATION

THE MACMILLAN COMPANY
NEW YORK • CHICAGO
DALLAS • ATLANTA • SAN FRANCISCO
LONDON • MANILA
IN CANADA
BRETT-MACMILLAN LTD.
GALT, ONTARIO

A Catholic Case Against SEGREGATION

Edited by Joseph E. O'Neill, S.J.

Foreword by Richard Cardinal Cushing

New York · *The Macmillan Company* · *1961*

Nihil obstat: Gall Higgins, O.F.M. Cap.
CENSOR LIBRORUM

Imprimatur: ✠ Francis Cardinal Spellman
ARCHBISHOP OF NEW YORK
July 26, 1961

The nihil obstat and imprimatur are official declarations that a book or pamphlet is free of doctrinal or moral error. No implication is contained therein that those who have granted the nihil obstat and imprimatur agree with the contents, opinions or statements expressed.

First Printing

The Macmillan Company, New York
Brett-Macmillan Ltd., Galt, Ontario

Printed in the United States of America

Library of Congress catalog card number: 61–16759

Foreword

Segregation is a sad stain which spreads across the fabric of America. We are now, surely, a long way past the time when we have to document the facts of discrimination or when we can question its unhappy effects on the American society. No longer is it necessary to go to books to find the stories of indignity, insult, hurt, and deprivation which have characterized the life of the Negro in America; our daily papers now carry constant news of these incidents because the Negro, at long last, has begun to make his protest heard.

Historians will have their problems explaining why a century was allowed to elapse between the time "the slaves were freed" and the true liberation of the Negro began to be accomplished. It would be interesting to catalogue the long list of excuses which otherwise fair and freedom-loving Americans allowed themselves in this context in order to explain inaction, postponement, and an undisturbed conscience. But looking back over the patent inadequacies of what has passed will not bring us very much closer to the day when discrimination gives way to brotherhood and men walk all together as sons of a common Father. Our day has its task cut out for it and we must be at it. These times call for the discovery and execution of effective means for ensuring that *every* civil right guaranteed by law is enjoyed by *every* citizen, whatever his race, creed, or color.

Nor is this just a problem for those who live in our southland. The American Negro population was once concentrated in a single area, but this is no longer true. Most of our large Northern cities and suburbs now have sizable colored groups among their citizens and there is ample evidence that prejudice and discrimination still follow the Negro to the north. Especially in the fields of housing and employment we must be prepared to take positive steps at once to see that race and color do not stand in the way of the rights and freedom of a whole group of Americans. We can no longer express ourselves in pious platitudes about human brotherhood and tolerance while we refuse to take straightforward action to correct these menacing social evils. Every day should mark some progress, and we should count that day lost in which we merely stand still.

I am pleased to recommend as a basis for intelligent action the essays in this book and I trust that those who read them will not merely be informed but inspired as well to move forward with vigor in ensuring social justice for all Americans.

In the last analysis, we will see the triumph of justice only when our hearts have been purified of all bitterness and our hands are ready to reach out to clasp in affection the hands of all our neighbors without concern for race, class, or color.

A few days ago I was told a story of two little girls who had spent their first day in an integrated school. One little Negro girl had entered the class that day and the place assigned to her was side by side with a little white girl. When the white girl returned home, her somewhat anxious mother asked her how everything had gone along at school. Her reply was impressive in its telling simplicity: "We were both so scared we didn't say anything to each other; we just held hands all day!"

The childlike way may be the clue we are seeking to find as our own way toward the solution of the problem of race discrimination in

America. Along with our plans and projects, our pleas and our programs, we must rediscover an authentic love for our fellow man from which all of these will take their vitality and finally be brought to success. Without this basic spiritual ingredient, no formula can possibly resolve our problem; with it our every effort will be blessed by God who is the Father of all men without exception.

RICHARD CARDINAL CUSHING
Archbishop of Boston

Introduction

Nearly a century and a half ago the great and grave question of slavery began to agitate this country in a way that can never be forgotten by Americans and should never be forgotten by other peoples. From the first timid cries of protest to the final Emancipation Proclamation by Abraham Lincoln on January 1, 1862, Americans thought and fought over the question, as fundamental as any for which men have suffered and died. Fanatics raged on both sides and temperate men pleaded for restraint, but the idea that slavery was morally wrong and should be abolished was slow in being appreciated by the human race, and was not fully accepted till long after this nation had exhausted itself in an agony of death and hate.

Yet the fact remains that only one side of the question was right. Slavery could not be both morally right and morally wrong. Why did so many people fail to see what seems so obvious to us today? Doubtless throughout the long history of slavery in various times and lands there were many reasons, but surely in the United States of the nineteenth century one of the strongest, apart from economic and cultural reasons, was that of ignorance based upon prejudice—irrational, ingrained, fostered. To break down and destroy so powerful a wall required time, action, and courage. For, as in all great questions of public morality, people were slow to admit the truth of what they did not want to believe. And they were even slower to accept with the emotions what their intelligence told them to be the truth. Consequently there had to be voices willing to speak out loudly, in public and in private, in season and out of season, and there had to be individual, concrete acts, first to dramatize the fact of the situation and then to live the reality of the point in question. Nothing else could have melted the icecaps of massive resistance created by the human will frozen to justice and charity. And only by actual living of the truth could the victory of the truth be made lasting. For it is not till the truth is actually lived that it is fully believed and able to structure the sinews of an entire society.

What was true of slavery a century and a half ago is true of segregation today. The issue is just as fundamental and just as explosive and there is only one side to the question. Segregation is wrong and should be abolished. Because the question is so vital and because the answer is being worked out slowly and painfully at this time, it is well to know the nature of the evil as fully as possible. With this end in view six important aspects of the question are discussed in this book. The first four were originally published in *Thought,* the quarterly of Fordham University, during 1960, the last three, together with the inspiring Foreword by His Eminence, Richard Cardinal Cushing, Archbishop of Boston, have been written especially for this publication. All are fundamental and necessary for a firm understanding of one of today's most pressing problems.

The first and most important aspect of all, as is the case with every great question of life, is the theological one. For if segregation is wrong it is wrong because it is immoral and not merely because it is undemocratic. It is the contention of the Reverend Robert W. Gleason, S.J., that compulsory segregation solely on the basis of race contradicts Revelation concerning the one origin, destiny, and redemption of the human person. It is therefore sinful, a violation of both justice and charity.

Segregation as a reality in America has a Constitutional history. It was not always thought of as undemocratic; it is so now. But the history of the practice as it was treated in the Supreme Court is a long one and progress toward its abolition was slow. The Reverend Arthur A. North, S.J., explains in graphic detail the Constitutional history and how with the death of the doctrine of "separate but equal" the Constitution became truly color-blind and so helped to bring about a new era of freedom under law.

The Reverend John W. Donohue, S.J., then takes a penetrating look at the historical record and the quasi philosophy of education which furnished the dubious ideological basis of the biracial public school system in the secondary schools in the South.

That we of the North may not be too hasty to condemn and too satisfied with the reality of our belief in equal rights for all, the Reverend Robert F. Drinan, S.J., examines with revealing results the actual working out of the process of desegregation by law in housing, education, and employment in certain cities and states of the North.

The Reverend Joseph H. Fichter, S.J., offers an authoritative sociological study of the remarkable contrast between the predictions, hopeful or dire, which people have made as to the certain consequences involved in the process of desegregation and what has actually occurred in each case.

Moving on into the area of psychology, Dr. Anne Anastasi presents a solidly factual and flawlessly argued thesis to the effect that educational segregation by race adversely affects the personality of the segregated group and inevitably leads to discrimination and to waste of human resources.

Finally, one of America's leading exponents, in theory and in practice, of interracial justice and charity, the Reverend John La Farge, S.J., after a realistic review of the entire situation, formulates out of his experience and wisdom the positive and constructive approach to the presence of the Negro in America as essentially and predominantly not that of a problem but of "a precious gift of the Creator to our nation."

It is the hope of all concerned in the making of this book that each of these essays may have some small share in the breaking down of the walls with which we Americans have too long surrounded ourselves!

JOSEPH E. O'NEILL, S.J.

Contents

A Catholic Case Against

SEGREGATION

The Immorality of Segregation

ROBERT W. GLEASON

I

A theological consideration of segregation is perhaps an unusual approach to this subject, but one that is demanded by its nature. The method of theology as a science varies from the method of philosophy or of pure science. Philosophy and natural sciences in the last resort demand as their basis facts which can be verified by experience or by reason. Theology, although it uses reason and is in fact a reasoned and ordered scientific expression of the Church's doctrine, in the last analysis relies upon the assertion of Revelation, the communication of God made to man in Scripture and tradition.

The premise from which theology starts is that God has intervened

in history to speak to man and that His assertions are immutably true,
governing principles for man's reflections upon them. It differs therefore from other rational disciplines by its method, that of authority.
The theologian's task is to discover the content of Revelation in Scripture and in tradition which the Church claims to guard and defend.
Thus to the nontheological mind theological method is frequently
shocking in its procedures. In no other science does a quotation from
authority cause an end to discussion. But in theology it does, if the
weight of the authority is sufficiently grave, and in the case of divine
authority, contained in Scripture and tradition, all argument ceases
once it has been rationally proved that Revelation has given a statement on the subject under discussion.

Thus the theologian's task is to discover what Revelation has said
explicitly and implicitly on the subject of segregation rather than to
marshal philosophical, economic, or any other type of factual argument. It is true that frequently what Revelation has to say will be
implicit and not explicit. It is also true that the weight of authority
varies considerably according to the authority cited. Thus, for example, a clear and open statement of Sacred Scripture, frequently
repeated, and easily verified by technical exegesis, has more weight
than does an authoritative statement of one of the Roman Congrega-
tions. Each one of these documents must be weighed carefully by experts to evaluate their content. The doctrine of a Roman congregation,
while in itself of less weight than an encyclical of the Holy Father
or a conciliar statement, may be of considerable weight simply from
the fact that it reflects a common teaching in the Church. Hence the
theologian is continually appealing to documentary evidence in a
fashion which is at least confusing to one who is not used to a method
which accepts as its starting point the fundamental belief that God
has intervened to communicate His mind to man in Revelation and,
as the Catholic Church believes, has established an infallible teaching body to interpret the Scriptures in which man finds God's assertions.

II

We may begin by observing that segregation is one form of the
philosophy of racism inasmuch as it implies a division and perhaps

a grading of human beings into different groups exclusively on the basis of race itself. This type of segregation sees man within a system of classification based exclusively on real or supposed genetic character. That such a doctrine stands in complete opposition to certain fundamental tenets of the Christian faith is what we shall attempt to establish.

Christianity and, as a matter of fact, the entire Judeo-Christian religion have certain fundamental convictions on the subject of the unity of the human race which are contradictory to any philosophy of race or segregation implying the human inferiority of any one race to another. Cultural inferiority there may possibly be, but what we are speaking of here is fundamental human nature as such, and the unity of the origin and of the destiny of man *as man.* Christianity has always insisted that mankind has taken its origin from the creative act of God who is *One,* and when St. Paul speaks of the universality of salvation offered to man by God he constantly recalls the unity of God Himself. It is upon such unity that he founds the unity of the human race and its one possibility of salvation. The prophets of Israel had insisted strongly upon the notion that the Lord God Yahweh is the omnipotent Lord of all peoples, even of those peoples who are outside that special providence which He had exercised over Israel. He is still the Lord of all and in time He will be manifested as such.

In the Christian tradition the Fathers of the Church hold a unique position. When they speak not merely as private Doctors but as witnesses to the faith of the nascent Church, and when with moral unanimity they hold a doctrine as certain, they are infallible interpreters of whether or not a point of doctrine is revealed.

Now it is quite evident that the Fathers of the Church take the story of Creation in the Genesis recital as manifesting the unity of all mankind in Adam and Eve, the first parents of the human race. The formation of Eve from Adam's body has as a dogmatic suggestion the affirmation of unity of all creation and the entire equality of human nature in man and woman and in all their descendants. This is also implied in the statement of God, "Let us make man in our image" (Gen.1:26). There is but one Godhead although the Christian faith affirms a trinity of Persons. Man is at the same time one and diverse. If individuals are considered he is many, but if the inner nature of man is considered, he is one, rational human nature with its essential characteristics being found in all races indiscriminately.

Christianity strongly affirms this unity at the origin of the human race and it also affirms its unity of destiny. The entire human race is moving under the guidance of God toward the term of history, the Resurrection of the eschatological Church, the final triumphant Church at the Parousia, the second coming of the Lord. Man was made one at the beginning and he will be one in the unity of the definitive Kingdom of God in heaven at the end. Jesus Christ is the instrument of God's plan to reunify all things in Himself and to empower human nature, the entire human family, to move toward this final unity. It is normal and just that humanity should develop a multiplicity of cultures and viewpoints, and this is quite possible within the unity of Catholicity. Thus, Christianity finds within itself the ability to combine the radical affirmation of one human race with a recognition of the diversity of races and cultures. Moreover, it attaches an importance to this diversity in that each race reflects differently, in its human and earthly values, the total perfection of God Himself. If man's unity from Creation is one and man's unity of destiny is one, this is but a corollary of the fact that man's nature is one.[1]

Human dignity is therefore the same in all men because all men have the same essential human prerogatives; they are all rational free beings with a divine destiny to which they are invited by God, namely, to participate in God's nature as nature, by grace freely given in this life and to experience the flowering of grace in the glory of eternity. Before Christianity certain philosophies, for example, stoicism, had recognized man's unity very clearly, but Christianity has placed this unity upon an absolutely certain basis because it has placed it upon the revealing word of God Himself to which man is called to make a free internal assent on the authority of God revealing. Because man had the same Creator and Father and the same Redeemer, he has also the same ultimate hope and vocation, the triumphant kingdom of the Church. As a result it is absurd to call upon our common Father in the Our Father, the prayer taught by Christ Himself, and at the same time to deny to a Negro, to a Chinese, or to a Jew the status of a brother. Even to imply a difference in status

[1] Yves Congar, *The Catholic Church and the Race Question* (Paris: Unesco, 1953), p. 202.

with regard to God would be implicitly to attack the Christian doctrine of the universality of God's paternal care and the common origin
and destiny of the human race. It is because there is one God and only
one God in whose image we have been created that we are all children
of the one Father and consequently that we are all brothers in Christ
in a way that no created power can assail. The only means of denying this common fact of brotherhood is to put oneself outside the universal paternity of God. The logical conclusion of this type of racism
is the abandonment of the Christian faith.[2]

Mankind also has a solidarity in sin in Adam and consequently
has a solidarity in the one mediator and Redeemer, Jesus Christ. St.
Paul asserts that there is one mediator between God and man. He is
the one who dies not for a single nation such as the Jews but for "all
men that they should be gathered together into one as children of
God" (John 11:52). There is no need for us to repeat the statements
of St. Paul on the universality of the redemption. Every statement
in Scripture concerning the redemption stresses its universality, the
fact that God has died for all men in Christ and consequently that all
men are united in the redemption of Christ and in the possession of
one mediator, Christ. From the viewpoint of Christianity all men have
the same vocation and they have the same essential history. This is of
course at a profound level since at the superficial level nations have
different histories but as human beings we all have the same history:
we were all created by God, fell in Adam, were redeemed in Christ,
and are moving in unity toward our term through history. We all
have also a common father in Abraham who became the father of all
nations at the call of God. Our history is recentered in Jesus Christ, the
universal Redeemer of all mankind, who proclaimed insistently the
equality and brotherhood of all men in Him under the Father. This
is why the Church has always proclaimed her unity and her Catholicity. The earthly body of Christ, the Church, must be one and there
can be no possibility of a national Church for each race or nation any
more than there can be the possibility of a different salvation or of a
different God for each nation or people.

It is true that there can be ethnic differences in rite and liturgy and
that there can be different jurisdictional groups based upon ethnic
division where this does not hinder the unity of the Church, but the

[2] Cf. Pius XI, "Mit brennender Sorge," *Acta Apostolicae Sedis,* 1937, p. 158.

Church herself is neither Latin nor Oriental nor white nor black. She adapts herself to all peoples and races and she does this by divine vocation. Were the Church to cease to operate in such wise as to unite all men of all races in herself, she would cease to be the authentic and Catholic Church of Christian Revelation. In adapting herself to man the Church can in no sense share in the divisions of men in such a way as to betray the spirit of the Gospel. The fact that the Church has been faithful to her divine vocation to unify all men within herself is evident from the continued accusations heaped upon her at every manifestation of racism in history. According to the racists the Church must be obliterated because she is determined upon world uniformity based upon a principle entirely different from that of race.

Pope Pius XII has given us a strong résumé of the unity of the human race from the viewpoint of Catholic doctrine: "It is a marvelous vision which makes one contemplate the unity of the human race in the unity of its origin in God, 'One God the Father of us all who is above all and who is in all things and in each of us' (Eph. 4:6), in the unity of its nature equally composed in all of us a material body and a spiritual, immortal soul; in the unity of its immediate end and of its mission in this world; in the unity of its dwelling place the earth, whose goods all men by right of nature can use to sustain and develop life, in the unity of its supernatural end which is God Himself to whom we must all tend and in the unity of the common means to attain this end" (Encyclical *Summi Pontificatus,* given the 20th of October, 1939).

The same Encyclical *Summi Pontificatus* proclaims in clear terms that "those who enter the Church whatever be their origin or language ought to know that they have an equal right of son in the home of the Lord." At the very peak of the fever of Nazism, Pius XII chose to put this doctrine into practice by elevating to the episcopate twelve priests from the far corners of the world and from diverse races. Pius XII further outlined the practical effects of unity in proclaiming that "the first of the pernicious errors which are spread abroad today is that of forgetting the law of solidarity, of charity dictated and imposed by the community of origin and by the equality of the reasonable nature in all men of whatsoever race" (Encyclical *Summi Pontificatus*).

At times a difficulty arises when one thinks of the Old Testament or even of certain expressions of Christ who proclaims that He has come first to Israel. But a second look at the situation makes us realize that neither the Old nor the New Testament has anything to say in favor of a theory of racism or of segregation. Doubtless Christ elected the Jews for a particular task but it is the racists who elect *themselves*, and without any sign of divine intervention in their favor arrogate to themselves a certain divine power. If Israel was chosen by God to be the object of His predilection, the Bible makes it eminently clear that Israel was chosen not because of her excellences but rather because of her weaknesses. It is the weak things of this world which God chooses to confound the strong. The racists, on the contrary, proclaim their pseudo-divine election by virtue of their qualities and excellences rather than their defects. Israel receives the task to bear witness to God even in difficulty and trials whereas the racists prefer to bear witness to themselves in triumph. This form of self-divinization is foreign to the prophets of Israel. Nor should one forget that Israel was opened to converts of good will and that her final destiny was to embrace all races of the earth and all the children of God. She was not closed in upon herself, as the racists are, guarding her prerogatives for herself. She was orientated toward an open future, toward the entire world, even though at times she was forgetful of this destiny and it had to be recalled to her, as St. Paul did repeatedly. "There are neither Jews nor Greeks" (Gal. 3:28).[3]

No Scripture scholar worthy of the name, Protestant, Jew, or Catholic, has attempted to find in the Old Testament anything which justifies enforced segregation based upon race. Considering the variety of interpretations which we meet among various Scripture scholars on most points, their unanimity on this point is quite striking. The Bible in no sense encourages segregation. There were certain laws among the Hebrews which forbade them to marry into other religions but this is a question of preserving the religious traditions of the people and not a question of preserving what we might call racial purity, a thing in which the Old Testament shows not the slightest interest. As a matter of fact, the Hebrews themselves were not a pure "race" but were the product of many different races. They inter-

[3] Cf. O. McGrath, O.P., "Theology of Race Segregation," *The Tablet* (London), April 13, 1951, reprinted *Catholic Mind*, Nov.–Dec., 1957, pp. 483–486.

mingled with many other people and their cultures were derived from their neighbors. The Old Testament offers us absolutely no suggestion that the chosen people attempted to remain racially "pure" or to propagandize racial "purity."

At times the biblical stories of Noah's sons and of the Tower of Babel have been interpreted as suggesting that God wanted separation of races and peoples. Historically this is absurd, since it is evident that language differences and racial differences existed long before any historical date that could be assigned to the accounts of Noah and of the Tower of Babel. Nor is there any suggestion in Sacred Scripture which accounts for the emergence of the colored race at these moments or suggests that the emergence of such a race was the result of a curse by God.

It is strikingly clear in the New Testament what was the attitude of Christ toward racial discrimination or discrimination based upon social inequality. Jesus always aimed at social unity and did nothing and said nothing which would encourage separation among people. He Himself was in fact accused of consorting with winebibbers and publicans, the most despised class in Israel. He insisted that we must treat each person as a neighbor, and the parable of the Good Samaritan is told to this point. He chose this as an example to teach people that the very type of person against whom the Jews, His listeners, had the greatest prejudices could be themselves more righteous than the Jews. There is no doubt that Jesus shocked his audience when he showed that the Samaritan in the story was a hero and that the Jewish people themselves were blameworthy because they did not treat their neighbor as a neighbor. This parable is peculiarly applicable to the question of race relationships because it is the very type of person whom the racists despise whom Christ would hold up to their admiration. In no place did Jesus intimate that we should indulge in racial purity or in class status. But He did insist very strongly that the final judgment would be largely based upon the question of how we have practiced love for our neighbor. He ordered us to love our neighbor as ourselves, and the theological reason for this is the physical mystical unity between Christ and the Christian. At no point did Jesus imply that love of our neighbor is without problems, is easy, or does not demand humility; but He never excused from this universal obligation.

In one place St. Paul counsels slaves to be obedient to their masters
and masters to be just and kind to their slaves. It is also true that St.
Paul taught quite clearly that in Christ there is no distinction between
slave and free man. St. Paul, the great Apostle of the Mystical Body
and the social unity of the Church, makes it very evident that the
greatest distinction existing in the Jewish world is abolished in
Christ, namely, the distinction between Jew and Gentile. "There is
neither Jew nor Gentile, free nor slave," he says (Gal. 3:28). We are
all one in Christ and we cannot therefore attack or suppress members
of another race.

III

The theologian who discusses the race question or the question of
segregation comes to it with a very definite background of Scripture
and tradition. To the theologian the unity of the human race based
upon its common origin in God, and its common destiny in God is so
clear that there can be no question of discussing whether or not one
race is inferior to another. Such a doctrine is simply theological
nonsense. It is from the background of his knowledge of the various
unities that bind men together whatever be their color or culture that
theologians deal with the concrete problems of segregation.

More than anything else, the Catholic Church has emphasized the
fact that our salvation is not individual but social. It is a salvation
which takes place within the interior of a social body, the Church. We
tend toward Christ as a *people,* the new people of God, in which all
distinction of color or culture is suppressed. Moreover, the Christian
is united with Christ and with every other Christian, every potential
member of Christ's Mystical Body as well as every actual member,
by many bonds. There is first of all this common natural solidarity
of possessing one and the same nature with all other men with no
essential distinction in one's human attributes. This is the basis of
human dignity as such in the purely natural order. Because each
man has the same human nature he has an ultimate dignity which
forbids that we treat him as anything less than man or that we impugn
this status of human dignity. He cannot therefore be treated as someone without an immortal destiny or without a spiritual soul, as an
animal. Beyond this unity in the natural order there is the unity

based upon God's creative providence which ushers all humanity as a unit toward a supernatural destiny. With the advent of the Son of God to assume human nature, humanity becomes even more unified because now God has inserted Himself in the human context of time and space and by adopting the same specific human nature as other men He has united all men in Himself. Moreover, theologians say that Christ held in unity in His human mind, by His knowledge of the beatific vision, all men past and present so that they are all united in this intentional unity in the mind of Christ. They are also all one in an affective unity because the will of Christ goes out with redemptive love to all members of the human race.

Moreover, in the supernatural order there is the institution of the Mystical Body, the Church, in which men are united to Christ by the physical bonds of sanctifying grace. Christ has established in His Church a prolongation of His Incarnation of which He is the head and we are the members. St. Paul has very strongly insisted upon this notion of the Mystical Body and St. John relates to us the parable, which Our Lord Himself chose to use, of the true vine and its branches in which all the members are united to one another because they are united to the head, the vine, that is, to Christ. Therefore any doctrine which assails these fundamental unities among Christians is an attack upon the Christian faith itself.

From such unities as this and from such principles as this theologians derive certain moral deductions.[4] This implies that morality does not depend upon custom or merely upon human legislation. Morality is of course something from within rather than something from without. It is a reflection of the entire nature of man in all his essential relations. A human act which conforms to the essence of man in all his essential relations is good and one which does not conform to his nature is evil. Rational human nature as such is therefore a norm of morality, and not custom or what society approves. The theory that whatever society approves becomes right has led to disastrous results in Nazi Germany.

Segregation based upon race alone, exclusively upon the title of race, clearly seems to violate man's obligations to his neighbor, obligations of both justice and charity. Compulsory segregation based

---

[4] Cf. Francis J. Gilligan, "Moral Aspects of Segregation in Education," *Proceedings of the American Catholic Theological Society*, 1958, p. 57.

exclusively upon title of race is an implicit denial of the equality of man and violates that law of human solidarity and charity which is imposed by our common origin and our common destiny as man. Because mankind is one society, descended from the common stock of Adam and with one common destiny, it follows that no man as man is inferior to another because of a particular race. There are inequalities of possessions, social status, talents, abilities, but there is no inequality in human dignity as such. Thus, to practice racial segregation in the belief that one is essentially superior to another because one is white or black or red, would be implicitly to deny the truth of the Catholic faith. The idea of white supremacy, when it involves this notion of an essential superiority of one race to another, is therefore an implicit attack upon some of the most fundamental attributes of the Christian faith. To believe that one nation or one race is essentially superior to another before God is evident error and should be recognized as such.

Even when the essential unity of the human race is not denied, compulsory segregation based exclusively on title of race can very easily involve other sins. For since we hold the essential unity of the human race, we hold also that men have conferred on them by God certain rights which we are bound to respect. Enforced segregation based exclusively upon title of race seems to us to be an attack upon the rights of the Negro as such. The moral basis for natural rights lies in man's intrinsic worth, in the dignity of his human person and in the sacredness of his destiny. Compulsory segregation violates the principles of justice because it restricts the free exercise of the natural right of the segregated. Personal individual liberty is interfered with without just cause, the right of the individual freely to choose the means for the complete development of his personality is denied him, and his dignity as a human being is humiliated when opportunities for work and associations with others are denied him. The individual has a right to be accepted on an equal footing with all other members of the human race insofar as his talents, his cultural abilities, and so on, permit. He cannot be excluded from the normal social contacts with other races by force. Even if segregation implies no discrimination, a thesis which we would admit with great difficulty, nevertheless, as long as it is compulsory in nature it violates justice because the basic human dignity of the Negro's person is thereby attacked, a stigma is forced upon the Negro by the white, and it is difficult to believe that it can continue long without further unjust treatment.

It is possible that segregation which was completely voluntary and completely without discrimination or inequalities could be admitted but even this, it would seem, is contrary to that bond of union and charity which should exist between people of the same country and the same region.[5] Compulsory segregation attacks the self-respect of the Negro himself because it presumes that there is within this race some essential reason why it should be roped off from the white race. In this there is implicitly suggested that the dignity of the Negro is inferior as a human person to the dignity of the white person. This inflicts an unjust degradation and an unreasonable humiliation upon the Negro and is incompatible with his human dignity. In addition, it makes it difficult for him to fulfill the demands of human personality by a social life which is in accord with that dignity. Consequently, the Church is opposed to all compulsory inequalities which keep the Negro from developing his human personality according to the dignity of his human nature.

IV

Christian moral theology recognizes that a man has a right to honor simply on the grounds of his humanity. To take away the honor which he deserves or, in other words, to insult someone seriously, can be a serious sin. When the Negro is treated in a way that implies an attack upon his basic human dignity, that is, with contempt and disdain, it is certain that an objective sin is committed, although frequently, because of ignorance or prejudice, in the subjective order, the sin may be only venial or light. We are also forbidden by Christian theology to entertain judgments or suspicions against others in which we accuse them of inferiority without reason. It sometimes happens that such an adverse judgment based upon insufficient reasons is sinfully lodged against the Negro. In the objective order such judgments without sufficient reason can become mortal sins.

Christians cannot approve of any policy which violates the law of love which is supposed to bind Christians together. Since all men are

[5] *Ibid.*, p. 56.

alike in their common human nature they ought to bear to one another charity and love, and Christ has said that to hate one's neighbors is contrary to the divinely revealed law of God. "Thou Shalt Love Thy Neighbor as Thyself." This love of neighbor from motives of faith and revelation is distinguished from the natural love which we are always obliged to give to the Negro in that it bases itself upon a good which has a direct supernatural reference to God Himself. In the concrete this good is the fact that an individual loves other men because they are children of God and reflect the perfections of God; he loves them in God for God. This precept of supernatural fraternal love is a serious one and must be taken seriously by Christians. We are required by it to love other people affectively, by wishing them well and by doing them good when the occasion arrives. Under all circumstances we are bound to love others, even when they have done wrong. We may correct them or punish them but we must still love other persons as persons. Any act of the will by which we deliberately set ourselves to oppose, out of hatred, what other people are attempting to do or frustrate their legitimate desires is undoubtedly a grievous sin. If emotional antipathy and aversion to the Negro become so strong that they involve positive contempt for the Negro person himself, this is objectively a sin. If this emotional aversion is so strong that it leads us actually to inflict harm upon him, we have obviously sinned against charity.

It is also true that Christian moral theology requires of every man that he give the common signs of friendship and consideration to other men. The omission of these "common signs," as they are called in moral theology, generally indicates contempt and gives reasonable cause for offense on the part of the Negro, which means that their omission is sinful. One cannot exclude the Negro from any group exclusively on the basis of race. For example, if all the members of an office are invited to a specifically "office" party, and a Negro who works in this office is excluded, solely because of his race, it is an offense against justice and the one excluding him commits an objective sin. White people are morally obliged to show to Negroes the common signs of courtesy and of fraternal love; to deliberately exclude them, solely on the basis of race, from these common signs would be a sin because it would attack the fundamental human dignity of the Negro and the fundamental law of Christian charity, and would be equivalent to showing contempt or hatred. It is possible that one could exclude the Negro from an office party on the grounds that he is individually an unpleasant person, if this could be proved reasonably, and that he would unduly upset the order of the party because of his individual personal characteristics. One could also exclude him for other reasons, for instance, that there would be no party if he were present, but the individual who would exclude him simply and solely because of his race would commit a sin.

Again with our neighbors, with our fellow workers, with our fellow citizens, we must employ the common courtesies. One need not admit them to personal friendship, but it is the duty of every Christian to extend to all the ordinary signs of courtesy. For example, if he says "good morning" to his white employees he should say "good morning" to his black employees; if he lunches with his white employees, he should not exclude from his luncheon table his black employee; if he shakes hands with white men he must shake hands with Negroes under the same circumstances. In individual cases the solution may be much more complex than that which I have indicated because there may be other principles involved. I have simply intended to underscore the general principle that one must extend to Negroes the same common courtesy which one extends to whites, and that one may not exclude them from social, political, and religious gatherings solely on the basis of their race. If, for example, a lawyer's club is formed and a Negro has all the requisites for joining this club, he may not be excluded on the basis of the fact that he is a Negro lawyer. Naturally one does not have to extend the courtesies of the club to people who are unreasonable, who create scenes, who are drunkards, who are scandalous, and so on, but one should not presume these defects in the individual, one must establish them before excluding him.

V

Racial segregation is therefore a sin contrary to the virtue of charity wherever it implies an exclusion from the common bond of love. Wherever it implicitly fosters hatred or contempt for the Negro, it is in opposition to the fundamental law of Christian charity. Compulsory segregation generally implies disdain and there is obviously some stigma imposed upon the one who is segregated or excluded.

Whether or not it leads to the unequal treatment of discrimination, compulsory segregation based exclusively upon title of race is seriously wrong. It is obvious also from the point of view of scandal that a serious sin may be committed. All have an obligation to avoid deeds or words which have the appearance of evil or which are occasions of sin for other persons. Now it is obvious that the Negro will not be attracted to the Christian Church by the un-Christian attitudes of certain white Catholics who attempt to exclude him from such activities as a common approach to the Communion rail, to a common meeting house, or to a common Church. This unreasonable attitude militates against the unity of the Church and her saving mission and is seriously wrong. Moreover, it frequently occasions, not unreasonably, in the Negro the suspicion that white Catholics do not appreciate the fundamental positions of their Church and fostering such a viewpoint in the Negro may be a sin in the objective order.[6]

Our conclusion, therefore, is that compulsory racial segregation based exclusively upon title of race implies the denial of the unity of the human race and the unity of its dignity in the natural and the supernatural order and implicitly contradicts the truths taught to us by philosophers and by Christian Revelation concerning the one origin, the one destiny, and the one redemption of the human person. It should have no place in a Christian's life. To hold that the white race is supreme or gifted by God with certain essential characteristics which the Negro race does not possess with regard to the essence of man would be a sin against Christ's revelation, against the Christian faith. We hold, moreover, that while it is theoretically possible that voluntary segregation which involves no inequality would not necessarily be gravely sinful, in practice it is almost impossible to conceive of such a situation, and even if such a voluntary segregation did exist it would not be the ideal, since it would tend to be contrary to the bonds of unity and love which should mark the Christian. We hold, moreover, that sins of injustice may frequently be committed by segregation of an enforced type based on race, that sins against charity may be frequently committed by such a type of segregation and that these sins may be grave.

Nevertheless the Church may tolerate segregation for a time, since

[6] Cf. J. Masson, "Le Chrétien devant le 'colour-bar'," *Nouvelle Revue Théologique*, 1956, p. 616.

prudence may dictate that the common good requires toleration in particular temporary situations. The duty of suppressing segregation may be subordinate to the common good at a particular moment in history. Perhaps at the present moment in certain cultures the common civil and Church good would be impaired if desegregation were to be forced upon an unwilling and uninstructed people. When this excusing cause operates, it operates only insofar as it protects the common good and *does not dispense from the obligation to do at once what can be prudently done* to remedy the evil. In personal relations, at least, justice and charity must be observed. In addition, the full truth must be taught to Christians on the position of the Church concerning the evil of segregation.

It will require patience and courage to complete the steps necessary to ensure the Negro his natural rights and to remove all stigma of inferiority. The problem of segregation results from centuries of inherited prejudice, and involves complex cultural patterns. Nevertheless, any "gradualism" which serves as a concealment for inaction or a plan to preserve the *status quo* must be done away with. It should be replaced with prudent advances which consolidate the gains of the past and prepare realistically for the future. Prudence does not imply inertia, but a wise choice of means adapted to an end toward which one works. Bitterness and hatred on either side are out of place. The segregation we now know seems a violation of commutative justice. Human beings are entitled to a certain honor and respect for their basic dignity and at present the Negro is often deprived of this. As Pius XII has said, "God did not create a human family made up of disassociated independent members. No: He would have them all united by a kind of total love of Him and consequent self-dedication to assisting each other to maintain that bond intact" (*AAS*, Sept. 7, 1956).

Hence, while the Church and civil society may tolerate evils for a while, each must recall the moral principles that govern delay in granting man his full natural rights. Ecclesiastical and civil administrators are guilty of an objective sin of injustice if they remain inactive or actively encourage involuntary segregation. Agitators or private individuals who encourage the perpetuation of segregation are also guilty of objective sin. Public peace and welfare demand that steps be taken with "all deliberate speed" rather than with a total and immediate solution but public peace and welfare cannot be invoked to promote segregation. Some delay may be warranted, provided one acts with sincerity, but history as well as moral theology warn us that protracted delay may not be tolerated. Involuntary segregation is not in conformity with the teachings of Christ. Consequently Christians must be instructed in this truth and must put aside all prejudice. Justice and charity must be stressed to the whites, patience and charity to the Negro.

The Plessy Doctrine: Rise and Demise

ARTHUR A. NORTH

In the complicated field of American politics there are certain political institutions which are almost synonymous with American government. Among these are popular sovereignty, federalism, separation of powers, and divided sovereignty. Although there exists in America a strong consensus regarding the general significance of these institutions, one will look in vain for an equally universal agreement concerning the political philosophy which underlies and supports them. The very creation of "a more perfect Union" spawned diverse and irreconcilable theories concerning the nature of that Union. There are some who believe that the Union was effectuated by the states in their governmental capacity; others maintain that the Union originated in and stemmed from the people of the United States, not as a composite mass but juridically organized within their several states. The former consider the Constitution of the United States as the beneficiary and creation of the existent state governments; the latter view it as the deliberate choice of the people acting in their sovereign capacity. By this choice the people, not the state governments, granted certain powers to the federal government, others to the state governments, and reserved still others to the states or to themselves.

The Constitution, therefore, even though it is the supreme law of the land, is not a grant of unlimited power. The framers in proposing and the people in ratifying it made a determined effort to limit the powers of the national government. One of the methods chosen to circumscribe these powers was the enumeration of the substantive powers granted. Consequently, a power which is not found among the enumerated powers nor among those reasonably implied or which is not a power possessed by the United States in common with the other nations of our international society, cannot be a power granted by the Constitution to the federal government. The ultimate foundation for this interpretation of the Constitution and its powers is the basic American theory that the people have a right to determine for themselves the form of government under which they wish to live.

That the power over or the control of education in the United States is not an enumerated power is certain. That such a power is not an implied power, except in a very limited area, is also quite clear. Yet the Supreme Court, one of the coordinate branches of the federal government, in interpreting a "constitution which has remained silent upon the matter of education, has exercised no little influence upon both the concept and the pattern of American education."[1] The instruments through which the Court has rendered articulate a Constitution educationally mute have been the Bill of Rights and Section One of the Fourteenth Amendment.

In three vigorously debated cases, the Everson,[2] McCollum[3] and Zorach,[4] the Court for the first time outlined its interpretation of the

[1] Spurlock Clark, *Education and the Supreme Court* (University of Illinois Press, 1956), p. 238.
[2] *Everson* v. *Board of Education,* 330 U.S. 1 (1947).
[3] *McCollum* v. *Board of Education,* 333 U.S. 203 (1948).
[4] *Zorach* v. *Clauson,* 343 U.S. 306 (1952).

"No establishment" clause of the First Amendment. In the first case, a sharply divided court, 5–4, sustained the constitutionality of a resolution of the township of Ewing, New Jersey, authorizing as a welfare measure the reimbursement of parents for the bus fares of their children who attended the public and parochial schools. In the second case the Court refused to sustain by an 8–1 decision the constitutionality of the Illinois system of "released time," which utilized the public school classrooms during the regular school hours for religious instruction given by priests, ministers, and rabbis. Four years later in a 6–3 decision the Court saw no constitutional violation in the "released time" program sponsored by New York State. In this program, unlike that of Illinois, the public school classrooms were not used and the State merely accommodated its school hours to allow children to attend religious instruction in their own churches. In these cases, the Court reached certain aspects of education through the religious liberty guarantees of the First Amendment, which was carried over as a restriction on state activity by the Court's interpretation of the word "liberty" in the Fourteenth Amendment. This action of the Court strengthened, according to its understanding, the so-called wall of separation between Church and State. In the cases dealing with segregation, the Court reviewed the entire field of education, even the "intangibles," and this time used both the "equal protection" clause of the Fourteenth Amendment and the "due process" clause of the Fifth Amendment to demolish the constitutional wall of segregation between the whites and the Negroes in the classrooms of America.

The seismic decision of the Supreme Court in the Brown case[5] on May 17, 1954, catapulted into national prominence a prolonged debate on basic principles of American government and American jurisprudence. This debate was carried on and developed simultaneously on three levels, historical, theoretical, and constitutional, with the Court as the focal point in the renewed discussion of American federalism.

For those who believed that it was a function of the Supreme Court in our federal system to midwife new social, economic, or moral ideas, sufficient precedents were found in the Court's role in implementing

---

[5] *Brown* v. *Board of Education of Topeka, Kansas,* 347 U.S. 483 (1954). *Briggs* v. *Elliott et al., ibid. Davis* v. *Prince Edward County School Board, ibid. Gebhart* v. *Belton, ibid. Bolling* v. *Sharpe, ibid.*

the social and economic policies of the New Deal. To this group the Court, in terminating segregation in public schools, merely completed the social revolution initiated by Franklin Roosevelt. For others who denied that the Fourteenth Amendment made the Supreme Court a "perpetual censor" of state laws and who maintained that the Constitution made adequate provisions through the amending process for rendering viable new social measures, the decision of the Court was a flagrant usurpation of powers reserved by the Constitution to the states. Historically and constitutionally, control of education had been considered one of the most important functions of state and local government. Americans have always thought and acted as if the public schools belonged to the local community. American education has been proud of its grass-roots traditions. For decades parents, either directly or through their representatives on the local school boards, have shared in the formation of public school policies, academic as well as administrative, and consequently, have determined in a significant manner both the education and associates of their children.

Segregation of the races in the South's public schools has been traditional in the United States. It has been the Southern educational way of life since the ratification of the Fourteenth Amendment. This practice had been sanctioned many times by state legislation, by decisions of the state courts and by those of the highest court in the land. "Somewhere, sometime, a counsel had argued, to every principle comes a moment of repose when the decision has been so often announced, so confidently relied upon, so long continued, that it passes the limits of judicial discretion and disturbances."[6]

American legal thinking along this line insists that the principle of *stare decisis* should have acted as a bar to the Court's reversing of well established precedents. The function of the Court is not to innovate but to protect and foster the dynamic equilibrium between nation and state. In this role the Court guarantees that "each will be sovereign with respect to objects committed to it and neither sovereign in respect to the objects committed to the other."[7] Proponents of this theory of the Court's role likewise object to what is considered the

[6] John W. Davis, *Oral Argument* in *Brown* v. *Board of Education* (private printing), p. 18.
[7] *McCulloch* v. *Maryland*, 4 Wheaton (U.S.) (1819) at 410.

Court's usurpation of congressional power. Section five of the Fourteenth Amendment authorizes Congress to enforce by appropriate
legislation the provisions of the Amendment. Since the people
neither directly nor through their representatives in Congress, had
taken any action to desegregate the public schools, it was considered
at least unwise for the Court in a democratic society to anticipate the
ballots of the people or to preempt the acknowledged domain of the
national legislature. That the Court was aware of these problems is
evidenced by one of the questions it submitted to the attorneys general of the states: "Is it within the judicial power, in construing the
Amendment, to abolish segregation in public schools?"[8] The ultimate
decision of the Court indicates that it felt it had, at least, concurrent
jurisdiction with Congress and since Congress had not acted, the
Court felt free to do so. Had the full meaning of the Fourteenth
Amendment been clarified by its consideration in Congress and by
its ratification by the states, perhaps the action taken by the Court
would not have generated so much confusion. As it stands, this initial
confusion was multiplied by several other conflicting factors in the
Brown case. In the first place, the Brown case actually included five
distinct cases. Four of these, since they dealt with state action, were
examined in the light of the "equal protection" clause of the Fourteenth Amendment. The fifth, *Bolling* v. *Sharpe*, originating in the
District of Columbia, in which the federal government has exclusive
jurisdiction, was decided on the basis of the Fifth Amendment, which
forbids federal activity "depriving any person of life, liberty or property without due process of law."

The necessity of interpreting two different amendments in order
to arrive at its unanimous nullifying decision, forced the Court to explain the relative significance of the "equal protection" clause of the
Fourteenth Amendment and the "due process" clause of the Fifth
Amendment. The explanation given by the Court to the effect that
these two clauses, although stemming from our American ideal of fair-
ness, yet were not always "interchangeable" and that "discriminations may be so unjustifiable as to be violative of due process"[9] was
not very enlightening. Furthermore, the constitutional criterion of
"due process" is "reasonableness." But six Courts prior to the War-

---

[8] *Brown* v. *Board of Education of Topeka, Kansas*, 345 U.S. 972–973 (1952).
[9] *Bolling* v. *Sharpe*, 347 U.S. 499 (1953).

ren Court had found state laws segregating the races in public schools reasonable means of achieving a legitimate governmental end. Only the Warren Court said such laws are "not reasonably related to any proper governmental objective."[10] What made these laws reasonable for all previous Courts but unreasonable to the Warren Court? Was it the "total view of education today"? Was it the sociological and psychological "predilection" of the Court? or was it "the felt necessities of the times, the prevalent moral and political theories," international and domestic, which induced the Warren Court to declare a hoary precedent unreasonable and discriminatory? That all these elements were somewhat intermingled with the Court's reasoning can hardly be denied. It is this intermingling of the disparate elements, employed by the Court to spell out discrimination, that has rendered the Brown decision subject to so much legal criticism.

In the realm of logic there are two other factors which have been productive of unnecessary confusion. The first stems from the Court's use of an analogy and the second originates in the implementing decision of 1955. In regard to the former, the Court transfers from the Sweatt and McLaurin cases an educational theory certainly applicable to graduate and law students and applies it to elementary and high school students where its applicability is not very evident. Speaking of educational factors necessary on a graduate level, like mutual interchange of ideas and group discussion with one's associates, Chief Justice Warren in the Brown case says "such conditions apply with added force to children in grade and high schools."[11] One may reasonably doubt the constitutional longevity of this bewildering judicial adaptation. Finally, the absence in the implementing decision of any discussion on the immediacy and personal nature of the right to education would seem to indicate that the Court was faced with more than a semantic problem in its search for equity.

Although the Brown case creates serious areas of doubt and confusion, the gradual refinement by the Court of the notion of equality required to sustain the Plessy doctrine leaves little room for doubt that the constitutional capsule, "separate but equal," was slowly but surely disintegrating and soon would be totally impotent in the field

10 *Ibid.* at 500.
11 347 U.S. 494 (1953).

of higher education. The demise of the Plessy doctrine was fore-shadowed by the Court's decision in the Gaines case.

II

The constitutional doctrine which guided the Supreme Court for fifty-eight years in its excursions into the field of segregated education was capsulized at an early date in the phrase "separate but equal." The doctrine originated not in a case concerning education but in one involving intrastate commerce, which lies, according to the Constitution, within the jurisdiction of the states. The state legislature of Louisiana in 1890 required railway companies, operating within the state, to provide equal but separate accommodations for the white and colored races. Mr. Plessy (⅞ Caucasian) refused to sit in a coach provided for Negroes and insisted upon being seated in the one for whites. He was arrested, tried, and convicted in the state courts for violating the law. Upon conviction he appealed to the Supreme Court of the United States to have the conviction set aside on the ground that the state law demanding separation of Negroes and whites on intrastate railways deprived him of his liberty without due process of law and in addition denied to him equal protection of the law in contravention of the Fourteenth Amendment.

Mr. Justice Brown, speaking for a majority of the Court, denied that the separate but equal accommodations required by law violated any section of the Fourteenth Amendment. He found the law of Louisiana a "reasonable exercise of the State police power"[12] and insisted that a state

... in determining the question of reasonableness is at liberty to act with reference to the established usages, customs, and traditions of the people, and with a view to the promotion of their comfort, and the preservation of the public peace and good order. Gauged by this standard, we cannot say that a law which authorizes or even requires the separation of the races in public conveyances is unreasonable, or more obnoxious to the Fourteenth Amendment than the Acts of Congress requiring separate schools for colored children in the District of Columbia, the constitutionality of which does not seem to have been questioned, or the corresponding acts of state legislatures.[13]

[12] *Plessy* v. *Ferguson* 163 U.S. 550 (1896).
[13] *Ibid.*

In view of the decision in the Brown case, 1954, it should be noted that the Court in this earlier case met and rejected the challenge of the due process clause by establishing the reasonableness of the Louisiana state law. The established usages, customs, and traditions of the people permitted no doubt in the Court's mind of the validity of the law demanding separate facilities. The Court did not agree with the thinking of some at that time that "laws requiring their separation . . . necessarily imply the inferiority of either race to the other."[14] Conversely, the Court noted that such laws "have been generally, if not universally, recognized as within the competency of the state legislatures in the exercise of their police powers."[15]

In the Plessy case the decision was not unanimous. There was a dissent and that dissent was made in rather vigorous terms by Justice Harlan. It was his opinion that the Louisiana statute was in violation of "the personal freedom of citizens."[16] To Harlan, the Fourteenth Amendment meant at least this:

That the laws in the States shall be the same for the black as for the the white. . . . and in regard to the colored race, for whose protection the amendment was primarily designed, that no discrimination shall be made against them by law because of their color.[17]

Separation of the races, by law on a railway, was unjust state discrimination, creating, as it did, "a badge of servitude wholly inconsistent with the freedom and the equality before the law, established by the Constitution."[18] Harlan maintained that the "Constitution was color blind, and, neither knows nor tolerates classes among citizens."[19] He expressed deep regret that a decision of the highest court in the land allowed a state to regulate the fundamental and personal rights of its citizens "solely upon the basis of race."[20]

As early as 1896, most of the charged elements which were thrust upon the Court in the Brown case were already present. The Court discussed the meaning of the Fourteenth Amendment; it looked into

14 *Ibid.* at 554.
15 *Ibid.*
16 *Ibid.* at 557.
17 *Ibid.* at 556.
18 *Ibid.* at 562.
19 *Ibid.* at 559.
20 *Ibid.*

the Civil Rights cases of 1883. It was conscious of the difference between political and social rights. It was not totally unaware of the psychological and social implications of the "badge of inferiority," which segregation might bestow.

The Court's reasoning in the Plessy case seems to have been strengthened by the fact that the laws in so many of the states in all parts of the country permitted or required segregation in public education. In establishing the doctrine of "separate but equal," the Court had fashioned a constitutional norm, a legal yardstick for measuring the validity of state statutes enforcing segregation of the races in intrastate transportation. The Court had within its judicial repertoire the means of transferring this norm as a constitutional test of enforced segregation in other fields. The means that the Court used was the simple but deceptive device of the analogical argument, a device used again by the Court in the Brown case of 1954, but perhaps, less convincingly.[21]

Perhaps "separate but equal" was one of those fortuitous phrases, such as "direct or indirect" or "business affected with a public interest," which from time to time extricated the Supreme Court from difficult positions but which the Court eventually has modified or discarded in the light of new experiences. Certain it is that "separate but equal" was the accepted constitutional solvent of racial problems from 1896 to 1954. Separatism in racial education is a relatively simple concept but the same cannot be said for the judicially accepted notions of equality. Commenting on the validity of the "separate but equal" principle, Professor Cushman said:

In common usage there are no degrees of equality, things or conditions are either equal or they are not equal. But the Supreme Court has not taken this view. It has held, rather, that equality in accommodations means not exact or mathematical equality, but only "substantial" equality. In earlier cases the Court was extremely lenient in construing what "equality" required in the segregated school system of the south. . . . It looked as though the Negro was not only to be segregated, but must also be content with very inferior accommodations and service under that segregation.[22]

[21] In the Brown case the Court by way of analogy applied educational methods designed for graduate and law students to elementary and high school children.
[22] Robert E. Cushman, *Leading Constitutional Decisions* (10th ed., New York, Appleton-Century-Crofts, 1955), pp. 182–183.

The force of Cushman's statement is clearly demonstrated in the first two cases directly concerned with the "separate but equal" doctrine in the field of public education. The Court seemed to have been more than lenient in its scrutiny of the "equality" of facilities offered to the segregated Negroes.

The first case to appear on the docket of the Supreme Court came on a Writ of Error from the Supreme Court of Georgia.[23] For several years, in accordance with the Constitution and statute laws of Georgia, the Board of Education of Richmond County had not only maintained by taxation a system of separate elementary-intermediate and grammar schools for all children but had also established several separate high schools.

Although the Georgia Act of 1872 did not authorize the Board of Education to establish a system of high school education, it did allow the Board at its discretion to establish "high schools at such points in the county as the interest or convenience of the people required."[24] The Board, in accordance with its discretionary powers, established in 1880 Ware High School for colored children. Seventeen years later, after a full hearing of all interested parties the Board for economic reasons closed Ware High School, the only public high school for Negroes. The Board claimed that this action was necessary to provide the "rudiments of education to two hundred Negro children" and that it was "financially unable at this time to erect buildings and employ additional teachers for the large number of colored children who were in need of primary education."[25] In the meantime, the Negro children of high school age and ability could attend, for a fee no higher than they were charged at Ware, any one of the three private colored high schools in Augusta.

Mr. Cumming and other interested Negro parents sought to enjoin the Board of Education from maintaining a high school for the white students while denying the same to Negro students. The parents "averred that the action of the Board of Education was a denial of equal protection of the laws secured by the Constitution of the United States."[26] Furthermore, they maintained, at the trial court, that it "was

23 *Cumming* v. *County Board of Education,* 175 U.S. 528–545 (1899).
24 *Ibid.* at 531.
25 *Ibid.* at 532–533.
26 *Ibid.* at 531.

inequitable, illegal and unconstitutional for the Board to levy . . . any tax for educational purposes of the county, from the benefits of which the petitioners in the persons of their children of school age were excluded and debarred."[27]

The trial court awarded an injunction restraining the Board of Education from using any tax-raised educational funds, present or future, to maintain a white high school until it provided "equal facilities" for Negroes, "or until further order of the Court."[28] However, the county trial court suspended its order to allow an appeal to the state's Supreme Court for an interpretation of the Acts of the State's legislature of 1872 and 1877, allowing the county school board discretion in establishing high schools at such points as the interest or convenience of the people required.

The Supreme Court of the state, after declaring that the "constitution and laws of that state justified the Board of Education in maintaining, at the expense of the plaintiffs, public schools for white children and in abolishing . . . similar or equivalent schools for the education of the colored children," reversed the judgment of the lower court on the ground "that it erred in granting an injunction."[29] In compliance with these instructions the trial court refused the relief asked by the plaintiffs and dismissed their petition.

It would seem worthy of note that in both the trial court and in the state Supreme Court the fact of separation of the races was not in contest and that the arguments centered on "equal facilities" and on whether the discretion allowed the Board of Education was "reasonable" or "arbitrary."[30] A review of the proceedings in the Supreme Court of Georgia would seem to indicate that the attorneys for the plaintiffs did not overemphasize the precise provisions of the Fourteenth Amendment they considered violated by the discretionary laws of Georgia. Furthermore, the plaintiffs' attorneys in the Supreme Court of the United States seemed more concerned with closing the high school for the white children than in opening one for Negroes. This fact was judicially recognized by Justice Harlan who wrote the opinion for the Court. In accepting the state Supreme Court's interpretation of its constitution and laws, Harlan said, in part:

[27] *Ibid.* at 532.
[28] *Ibid.* at 535.
[29] *Ibid.* at 536.
[30] *Ibid.* at 538.

Under the circumstances disclosed, we cannot say that this action of the State Court was, within the meaning of the Fourteenth Amendment, a denial by the State to the plaintiffs and to those associated with them, of the equal protection of the laws or of any privilege belonging to them as citizens of the United States. . . . The education of the people in schools maintained by state taxation is a matter belonging to the respective states, and any interference upon the part of the federal authority with the management of such schools cannot be justified except in a case of a clear and unmistakable disregard of rights secured by the Supreme Law of the land.[31]

It is of no little significance that the decision in this case was unanimous and that it was announced by the justice who in the Plessy case claimed that the "Constitution is color blind."

Twenty-six years were to pass before the next case involving the "separate but equal" doctrine in the field of public education came before the Supreme Court of the United States. The intervening period, although generally one of calm, was not without its race problems in education and transportation. These conflicts, however, were resolved in the various states and lower federal courts by the Plessy formula and the Cumming precedent. Why, then, did the Court choose to hear its second case on segregated education in the conflict of *Gong Lum* v. *Rice*?[32] Perhaps the answer to this question may be found in the fact that Martha Lum, in whose interest the Constitution and statute law of Mississippi were challenged, happened to be an American citizen of pure Chinese descent. For her, as well as for the Negro, race and the color line barred her admission to the white school of her choice. The Negroes, however, were somewhat more fortunate, for they had schools of their own but there was no school in the state for the Chinese. The state Supreme Court was unable to grant Miss Lum the desired relief because the "constitution divided the educable children into those of the pure White or Caucasian races, on the one hand, and the Brown, Yellow and Black races on the other."[33] In view of this constitutional division of the races the court saw no necessity for the state legislature to provide separate schools for each race. Miss Lum, it was clear, was entitled to all the benefit of the colored public schools.

[31] *Ibid.* at 545.
[32] *Gong Lum* v. *Rice*, 275 U.S. 78–87 (1927).
[33] *Ibid.* at 82.

The Supreme Court of the United States experienced no difficulty in affirming the decision of the state courts. Speaking through Chief Justice Taft, a unanimous court said:

The question here is whether a Chinese citizen of the United States is denied equal protection of the laws when he is classed among the colored races and furnished facilities for education equal to that offered to all, whether White, Brown, Yellow or Black. Were this a new question it would call for a very full argument and consideration but we think that it is the same question which has been many times decided to be within the constitutional power of the state legislature to settle without intervention of the federal courts under the federal Constitution.[34]

The Court in this case as well as in the previous one did not seem to have been overly concerned with any specific test of equality. It almost seems as though the Court assumed that the separate education was equal. Having satisfied itself that there was a school for the colored race and that it was situated in a convenient place for Martha Lum, the Court did not, as far as the records show, question the equality of the two schools in regard to physical facilities, curriculum or length of the school term. In ths case the Court accepted, *sub silentio,* a new development in regard to separation, that is, that separate education meant that only whites are to be segregated. The commingling of the Negroes with the other races presented no constitutional bar to the Plessy doctrine of "separate but equal."

The laissez-faire attitude of the Court toward the genuine equality of segregated education underwent a change in the Gaines case[35] and this decision has been considered by some as "a landmark in the history of Negro education."[36]

The State of Missouri had provided by law for the separation of Negroes and white students in education. It had made great strides in equalizing the facilities for each. The University of Missouri was established for whites, and Lincoln University for Negroes. Although a Negro could not attend the law school of the University of Missouri, the state did guarantee by law a legal education to those Negroes

[34] *Ibid.* at 85–86.
[35] *Missouri ex Rel. Gaines* v. *Canada, Registrar of the University of Missouri et al.,* 305 U.S. 337–354 (1938).
[36] Spurlock, Clark, *op. cit.,* p. 190.

who desired it. Mr. Lloyd Gaines, a well qualified graduate of Lincoln University, applied for admission to the law school of the University of Missouri. The University denied him admission "on the ground that it was contrary to the constitution, laws and public policy of the State to admit a Negro as a student in the University of Missouri."[37] Although Mr. Gaines did not test the Missouri law by applying for admission at Lincoln University and in this manner failed to avail himself of all administrative procedures, he claimed that the refusal on the part of the University of Missouri to admit him as a law student constituted a "denial by the state of the equal protection of the laws in violation of the Fourteenth Amendment of the Federal Constitution."[38]

Mr. Gaines initiated a mandamus proceeding to compel the Curators of the University to admit him. The Circuit Court of the state refused to grant the writ and its denial was sustained by the Missouri Supreme Court. The Supreme Court of the United States granted certiorari.

In argument before the Supreme Court the Curators maintained that the state had not denied the plaintiff equal protection of the law. To substantiate this claim, they appealed to the Missouri statute which allowed the curators of Lincoln University discretionary powers either to establish a law school for Negroes or to pay the tuition of the qualified Negroes who wished to attend law schools in one of the adjacent states. These law schools in Kansas, Nebraska, Iowa, and Illinois, the defendants insisted, were the equals of that of Missouri. The same system of education was used in all. All the law schools, including that of Missouri, trained students for the practice of law in any state where the Anglo-American system of law obtains. Even the case books used in all five schools were substantially identical.

Mr. Gaines, however, pointed out that regardless of these similarities there were other very important and definite advantages in attending law school in Missouri, such as studying Missouri law, attending Missouri's courts, and the prestige of the Missouri Law School in Missouri where his future clients would live.

The Supreme Court of the United States refused to accept the defendant's arguments as pertinent and reversed the decision of the Su-

[37] 305 U.S. at 343.
[38] *Ibid.* at 342.

preme Court of Missouri. Chief Justice Hughes, speaking for the Court, said:

> The basic consideration is not as to what sort of opportunities other states provide, or whether these are as good as those in Missouri, but as to what opportunities Missouri itself furnishes to white students and denies to Negroes solely on the ground of color. The admissibility of laws separating the races in the enjoyment of privileges afforded by the state rests wholly upon the equality of privileges which the laws give to separated groups within the state. . . . The equal protection of the laws is a pledge of the protection of equal laws. . . . Manifestly, the obligation of the state to give the protection of equal laws can be performed only where its laws operate, that is, within its jurisdiction.[39]

The Court was also unwilling to accept the state's plea that the legal education it provided outside the state was only temporary until Lincoln University had time to establish a law school. This "resort" the Court said, "may mitigate the inconvenience of the discrimination but cannot serve to validate it."[40]

This case is significant for at least two reasons. In the first place, the Court was not willing to accept nominal equality as a justification for segregated education. As a matter of fact the Court refused to approve of substantial equality supplied by another state. Secondly, it is of no little importance that the decision of the Court in this case was announced by Chief Justice Hughes. Twenty years prior to this decision, Mr. Hughes, then an associate justice, had spoken for the Court in a case concerned with interstate commerce and segregation.[41] At that time, he rejected as immaterial a railway company's rebuttal that the reason why equal but separate accommodations, sleeping and dining cars, had not been provided for Negro passengers, was the fact that few Negroes traveled on the line. Mr. Hughes said:

> This argument with respect to volume of traffic seems to us without merit. It makes the constitutional right depend upon the number of persons who may be discriminated against, whereas the essence of the constitutional right is that it is a personal one.[42]

[39] *Ibid.* at 349–350.
[40] *Ibid.* at 350.
[41] *McCabe* v. *Atchinson, T. & S. F. Ry. Co.* 235 U.S. 151–161 (1914).
[42] *Ibid.* at 161.

Mr. Hughes, now Chief Justice, in the Gaines case, again and on the identical ground, refused to accept Missouri's reason for not providing a law school in Missouri for Negroes, because there was not a sufficient number of requests from Negroes. The right of Mr. Gaines for a legal education provided by the state of Missouri, Mr. Hughes said, "was a personal right."[43]

While the Chief Justice did not maintain that the state had a duty to provide legal training for its citizens, he did insist that it was the state's duty to provide equal facilities for Negroes, if the state offered legal education for the whites. It was, the Court said, "as an individual that he [Gaines] was entitled to the equal protection of the laws, and the state was bound to furnish him within its borders facilities . . . whether or not other Negroes sought the same opportunities."[44]

The judicial transfer of the personal element of the constitutional right from the McCabe, an interstate commerce case, to that of Gaines, an education case, reoriented the notion of equality in the Plessy doctrine of "separate but equal." As a result of this decision the Court demanded not only that separate education be equal and that this equality be established within the state concerned but also it indicated, because of the personal nature of the right involved, that it would not tolerate a delay on the part of a state in creating equal facilities for even one Negro student.

This decision, although still honoring the Plessy doctrine, actually sounded the death knell of the separate but equal philosophy in graduate and professional education. To establish for one, two, or even a few Negro students professional and graduate schools, which would be equal to the time-honored universities of the South, would be no easy task, even though the South might try it. The thinking, however, in the Gaines case left separate education no other alternative. Even this alternative was restricted by the first case to come before the Supreme Court after World War II, *Sipuel* v. *Board of Regents.*[45]

The case arose in 1946. The University of Oklahoma, although it provided no law school for Negroes, refused, solely because of her

[43] 305 U.S. at 351.

[44] *Ibid.* at 351.

[45] *Sipuel* v. *Board of Regents of the University of Oklahoma et al.,* 332 U.S. 631 (1948).

color, to admit Ada Sipuel as a student. Miss Sipuel requested the district court to issue a writ of mandamus, compelling the school authorities to admit her. The district court refused to comply and its refusal was confirmed by the state Supreme Court. The Supreme Court of the United States granted certiorari and in a *per curiam* decision announced another significant point of law which rendered the state's defense of the separate but equal doctrine still more difficult. The Supreme Court issued the following mandate:

The petitioner is entitled to secure a legal education afforded by a state institution. To this time, it is denied her although during the same period many white applicants have been afforded legal education by the state. The state must provide it for her in conformity with the equal protection clause of the fourteenth amendment and *provide it as soon as it does for* applicants of any other group.[46]

In an all-out effort to comply with the Court's mandate and at the same time to preserve segregation in legal education, the University's regents announced that Langston University, the state Negro college, would open a law school for Miss Sipuel. This law school, created on the spur of the moment, consisted of three white lawyers who were assigned to teach Miss Sipuel in a room in the state Capitol. Miss Sipuel declined the offer and began legal proceedings to gain admission to Oklahoma University's law school. She denied that the creation of her three-professor law school met the demands of the Court's mandate. Before her appeal had reached the Supreme Court, which was soon by another *per curiam* opinion to deny her contention, Miss Sipuel had become Mrs. Fisher. In 1949 the University of Oklahoma, free from all legal compulsion, admitted Mrs. Fisher for the study of law.

Perhaps the gratuitous act of the university was not without a tinge of self-interest. Mrs. Fisher had not been the only one who thought that the spontaneous creation of a three-professor law school was an evasion of the Court's mandate. Mr. Justice Rutledge dissenting in the Fisher case said:

In my judgment neither the action taken by the Supreme Court of Oklahoma nor that of the District Court of Cleveland County, following upon

[46] *Ibid.*, 631–632.

the decision and issuance of our mandate in Sipuel v. Board of Regents, 332 U.S. 631, is consistent with our opinion in that case or therefore with our mandate which issued forthwith.[47]

It would be difficult to find any substantial equality in the separate school of three professors and one student. But for the time being, at least, the Court seemed willing, although there were two justices dissenting, to accept this miniature law school as meeting the requirements of "separate but equal" and as satisfying the personal element of the right to equal protection of the laws. Two years later, however, the Court made a more serious effort to guarantee the Negroes "equality in fact and not in legal fiction."[48] In *Sweatt* v. *Painter*[49] the Court turned the searchlight of judicial review on the two remaining but judicially weakened ramparts of the wall of segregation in the field of higher education.

The Sweatt case had many points in common with those of Sipuel and Fisher. Mr. Sweatt was denied admission to the University of Texas law school on the sole ground that he was a Negro and that the University was for white students only. At the time of his application for admission there was no law school for Negroes in Texas. Mr. Sweatt initiated mandamus proceedings but the trial court, although it recognized that the state's action in denying him an opportunity for legal education granted to others was a deprivation of his rights guaranteed by the Fourteenth Amendment, did not allow the relief requested. As a matter of fact, it continued the case for six months to allow Texas time to establish a law school for Negroes. This law school was not much better than that established by Oklahoma for Miss Sipuel. It had no independent full-time faculty or library. It was not accredited. Mr. Sweatt refused to enroll and the trial court denied the writ of mandamus on the finding that the new Texas law school for Negroes was substantially equivalent to that offered by the state to white students. The Supreme Court of Texas refused to hear an appeal but the Supreme Court of the United States granted it.

In the meantime the State of Texas increased the facilities for the

[47] *Fisher* v. *Hurst,* 333 U.S. 151 (1947).
[48] *Ibid.* at 152.
[49] *Sweatt* v. *Painter,* 339 U.S. 629 (1950).

Negro law school. It now had a faculty of five full-time professors, a student body of twenty-three, over sixteen thousand volumes in a library served by a full-time staff, a legal aid society, and was well on the way to full accreditation. The Supreme Court of the United States looked for but was unable to find substantial equality between the Negro law school and that provided for whites by the University of Texas. The latter had a larger full-time faculty, many of whom were recognized authorities, a voluminous library, a large student body, a law review, moot court facilities, and very distinguished alumni. As a result of this comparative study the Court declared:

> We cannot find substantial equality in the educational opportunities offered white and Negro law students by the state. . . . What is more important, the University of Texas Law School possesses to a far greater degree those qualities which are incapable of objective measurement but which make for greatness in a law school. Such qualities, to name but a few, include reputation of the faculty, experience of the administration, position and influence of the Alumni, standing in the community, tradition and prestige.[50]

In view of the evident inequalities the Court, relying on its determination of the "immediacy" of the petitioner's right to equality in the Sipuel case and the personal and individual nature of that right, previously stressed in the Gaines case, declared:

> we hold that the equal protection clause of the fourteenth amendment requires that the petitioner (Mr. Sweatt) be admitted to the University of Texas Law School. The judgment is reversed.[51]

This decision all but shattered the wall of segregation in the field of higher education provided by a state. This was the first time that the Supreme Court directed a law school reserved for white students to admit a Negro. While it must be admitted that the Court did not say that no state law school established for Negroes could be equal to that of a long and well established state law school for whites, the implications of such an impossibility were clearly visible. It must also be conceded, especially in view of the Court's refusal to reexamine the Plessy doctrine, that separate education remained within

[50] *Ibid.* at 633–634.
[51] *Ibid.* at 636.

the meaning of the Fourteenth Amendment as long as such education was equal.

The McLaurin case,[52] decided at the same time as that of Sweatt, made the realization of substantial equality more difficult by rejecting a rather simple form of segregation. Mr. McLaurin, an experienced Negro professor with a master's degree, sought admission to the graduate school of the University of Oklahoma to study for his doctorate in education. On being denied admission solely because of his race, he sought injunctive relief "alleging that the action of the School authorities and the state statutes upon which their action was based, were unconstitutional and deprived him of the equal protection of the laws."[53] A three-judge district court, adhering to the doctrine of the Sipuel case, held that the state had a duty to provide Mr. McLaurin with the education he sought as soon as it provided it for others, and, in addition, that Oklahoma's statutes, inasmuch as they were the legal basis for excluding the plaintiff, were unconstitutional. Despite this judgment, the Court refused to grant the relief requested on the presumption that the State of Oklahoma would obey the constitutional mandate. The legislature of the state did alter its statutes to admit Negroes to institutions of higher learning in specified cases. However, the amended statute still required that such Negroes as were admitted to state institutions reserved for whites were to be given instruction "upon a segregated basis." The concrete manner of segregation was left to the "discretion of the president of the University."[54]

In accordance with the amended Oklahoma statute and the discretionary decree of the president of the university, Mr. McLaurin was required:

. . . To sit apart at a designated desk in an anteroom adjoining the class room; to sit at a designated desk on the mezzanine floor of the library, but not to use the desks in the regular reading room; and to sit at a designated table and to eat at a different time from other students in the school cafeteria.[55]

[52] *McLaurin* v. *Oklahoma State Regents for Higher Education et al.,* 339 U.S. 637 (1950).
[53] *Ibid.* at 638–639.
[54] *Ibid.* at 639.
[55] *Ibid.* at 640.

Mr. McLaurin filed a motion to modify these conditions but the district court, which had retained jurisdiction in the case, denied that this form of segregation was a denial of the equal protection of the law. An appeal was carried by the plaintiff to the Supreme Court of the United States. However, before this appeal was heard, the university altered the treatment of the plaintiff. Under the revised system he was allowed to sit in the same classroom but in a row specified for colored students; he was permitted to eat at the same time in the cafeteria but only at a special table; he was assigned to a table in the main library.

On a review of this case the Supreme Court was of the opinion that even these so-called minor restrictions seriously impeded the plaintiff's ability "to study, to engage in discussion and exchange of views with other students, and, in general, to learn his profession."[56] The Court considered as irrelevant the defendant's argument that the students themselves, even though the school's restrictions were removed, would refuse to associate with Mr. McLaurin. The Court went on to say:

There is a vast difference, a constitutional difference between restrictions imposed by the State which prohibit the intellectual commingling of the students, and the refusal of individuals to commingle where the state presents no such bar.[57]

The Court seemed fully aware, in view of the increasingly complex nature of our society, that the impairment of Mr. McLaurin's education would be reflected in that of all who were later to study under his guidance. In conclusion Chief Justice Vinson, citing the Sweatt case and speaking for the Court said:

We conclude that the conditions under which this appellant is required to receive his education deprive him of his personal and present right to the equal protection of the laws. We hold that under these circumstances the fourteenth amendment precludes differences in treatment by the state based on race. Appellant, having been admitted to a state supported graduate school, must receive the same treatment at the hands of the state as students of other races. The judgment is reversed.[58]

56 *Ibid.* at 641.
57 *Ibid.* at 641.
58 *Ibid.* at 642.

The Court's decision in the McLaurin case marks the end of an era. During the fifty-four years since the announcement of the Plessy doctrine the Court had modified its definition of equality case by case. It was satisfied in the beginning with a nominal equality, separate classrooms or buildings, without very much concern for curriculum or school term. As a matter of fact, an examination of the early cases would almost lead one to believe, at least as far as the Court was concerned, that education in the South, since it was separate, was presumed to be equal. Furthermore, with the exception of Hughes during his first appointment to the Court, no one seemed to have realized that the equality guaranteed by the Fourteenth Amendment was a personal right and that a delay by state action of its implementation was a violation of the constitutional right.

The return of Hughes in 1930 to the Court, this time as Chief Justice, coupled with the social and economic revolutions of the thirties, was a significant event. Nor is it of less significance that the Gaines case came before the Court after the Roosevelt attack on the Court and after Hughes had converted one of the Court's five conservatives and carried him along with the majority in the epoch making decision in a civil and social rights case.[59]

Nominal equality yielded in the Gaines case to a substantial equality which became more concerned with the total view of modern education just as the West Coast Hotel case had taken a total view of the position of women not only in the economy but also in the life of America. According to this new view of equality in education, similar classrooms, matching curricula, qualified teachers were not sufficient to justify separation.

III

Between the decision in the Gaines case and the next case involving the question of segregation in education, the Second World War had been fought. In this war Negroes had served their country well not only in the labor fields on the home front but also in the various branches of the service. In the postwar years, many economic and social developments had been achieved. Along with these developments came a new equality, the equality of opportunity for all. This

[59] *West Coast Hotel Co.* v. *Parrish,* 300 U.S. 379 (1937).

equality was in no little way based on the recognized need for and expansion of education. Education for all became a slogan. In an attempt to overcome existing bias in the basic fields of American life, President Truman by an executive order[60] established a Civil Rights Committee and shortly thereafter prohibited segregation in the armed forces. Consequently, by the time that the Sweatt and the McLaurin cases were heard by the Supreme Court, a new social and political milieu had been created. One is not surprised, therefore, to find the Court's new definition of equality in educational facilities reflecting the effects of the great social change. In these cases also, the Court emphasized the fact that the right to these facilities was a personal and an immediate one.

Three of the post-World War II cases were concerned with law school education. The Supreme Court needed no extrinsic norms to inform itself on the constituent elements of legal education. The Court is a group of lawyers. They knew that a law school needed more than a classroom building and a library. Interchange of ideas, association and discussion among law students were also essential for their development. Moot courts and attendance at the trials of the local Bar were as important as renowned professors, a law journal, and distinguished alumni. Many of these elements defied objective measurements and were intangible but their presence, the Court said, "makes for greatness" in law school education. No separate makeshift law school could meet these demands or possess the equality necessary for separateness. These ideas, reinforced by Hughes's precedents in *McCabe* v. *Atchison* and *Sweatt* v. *Painter*, opened the doors of the white law schools for qualified Negro students. The McLaurin case played a similar role for the Negro graduate students. Here separateness, segregation in itself, was revealing its basic inequalities. Had the Brown case involved legal and graduate education, few students of the Court or of education would have been surprised or shocked at the Court's rejection of the "separate but equal" doctrine.

By a continual refinement of its definition of equal facilities, the Court, in deference to its traditional reluctance to consider constitutional issues, except in the particular case at hand, had been able since 1896 to find in all cases inequalities and consequently was not forced by the existent facts of any case to reexamine the Plessy doc-

[60] Executive Order 9808, Dec. 5, 1946.

trine. However, by 1952, five[61] cases had reached the Supreme Court, one of which, by its facts,[62] and all by the urging of counsel, demanded a reexamination of the separate but equal doctrine in the light of the total concept of modern education.

We must consider, the Court said, public education in the light of its full development and its present place in American life throughout the nation. Only in this way, can it be determined if segregation in public schools deprives these plaintiffs of the equal protection of the laws.[63]

The cases which are known as the Brown case had their origins in the states of Kansas, South Carolina, Virginia, Delaware, and the District of Columbia. Although these cases differ somewhat both in regard to their facts and local conditions, a common legal question, the Court said, "justifies their consideration together in this consolidated opinion."[64]

Each case was concerned with minors of the Negro race who had been denied by public authority admission on a nonsegregated basis to the public high schools of their respective communities. In all cases but that of Delaware, a three-judge Federal district court denied relief to the plaintiffs on the ground of the familiar "separate but equal" principle of the Plessy case.

Members of the National Association for the Advancement of Colored People, attorneys for the plaintiffs, taking their lead from the Kansas case contended that compulsory segregation by race in public school education was in its very nature an unjust discrimination and, consequently, such education was not and could not be equal. On the district court level in *Brown* v. *Board of Education of Topeka, Kansas,* the Court found that

Segregation of white and colored children in public schools has a detrimental effect upon the colored children. The impact is greater when it has the sanction of law for the policy of separating the races is usually interpreted as denoting the inferiority of the Negro group.[65]

[61] See note 5 above.
[62] 347 U.S. at 492 footnote 9.
[63] *Ibid.* at 492–493.
[64] *Ibid.* at 486.
[65] *Ibid.* at 494.

The Court was also of the opinion that compulsory segregation led to the retardation of the educational and mental development of Negro children. This finding was in full agreement with that of the Court in *Gebhart* v. *Belton* in which it said:

I conclude from the testimony that in our Delaware society, state-imposed segregation in education itself results in the Negro children, as a class, receiving opportunities which are substantially inferior.[66]

Before the Supreme Court rendered its decision in the Brown case, it restored all the cases to the docket for further argumentation on five[67] specified points, some historical, others legal, and others concerned with judiciary equity. It invited the Attorneys General of the United States and of the Southern states as friends of the Court to file briefs answering the proposed questions. The briefs of the Southern states presented a unanimous opinion that the Congress which passed and the states which ratified the Fourteenth Amendment did not intend the abolition of segregation in public schools. The National Association for the Advancement of Colored People, whose attorneys acted for the Negro children, also filed a brief in which it was alleged that it was evident that both the Congress and the ratifying state conventions intended the abolition of segregation in public education. The brief, however, of the Attorney General of the United States claimed that history on this precise point was not conclusive. The Court, in the light of this contradictory testimony, while admitting that the historical findings "cast some light"[68] on the point in issue, concluded that "it was not enough to resolve the problem with which we are faced. At best, they are inconclusive."[69]

Similar conflicting findings were presented to the Court on the second question, with the Attorney General of the United States and the attorneys for the colored children answering the third question in the affirmative, namely, that "it was within the judicial power in construing the amendment to abolish segregation in public schools."[70]

[66] *Ibid.* at 494 footnote 10.
[67] 345 U.S. at 972 (1952).
[68] 347 U.S. at 489 (1953).
[69] In the Supreme Court of the United States, October Term 1953, Brief for Appellants in Nos. 1, 2, and 4, and for Respondents in No. 10, on reargument, pp. 17, 18.
[70] 345 U.S. at 972 (1952).

Since the Court found the historical argument concerning the meaning of the Fourteenth Amendment inconclusive, it refused to "turn the clock back" to 1868 and directed its attention to a consideration of public education "in the light of its full development and its present place in American life throughout the nation."[71] The Court recognized the fact that education was perhaps the most important function of state and local governments. It found evidence to sustain this conclusion in the compulsory school laws and the great expenditures of the various states, in the fact that education is necessary for an understanding and fulfillment of our most basic public responsibilities, for competent service in the armed forces, and for intelligent citizenship.

After a thorough review of the importance of education for a democratic society, for the awakening of cultural values and of their need for successful living, the Court took judicial cognizance of the social, psychological, and educational effects of segregation on the growing child. It found that even where physical facilities and other tangible factors were equal, racial segregation "deprived the children of the minority group of equal educational opportunities."[72] The Court accepted the opinion of the social scientists that racial segregation breeds a sense of inferiority in the colored child; that it impairs the learning process and does, perhaps, irreparable injury to the hearts and minds of the children. In the light of the vast importance of education in America and the psychological traumas effected by segregation solely upon the basis of race, the Court concluded that:

In the field of public education the doctrine of separate but equal has no place. Separate facilities are inherently unequal. Therefore, we hold that the plaintiffs and others similarly situated for whom the actions have been brought are, by reason of the segregation complained of, deprived of the equal protection of the laws guaranteed by the Fourteenth Amendment.[73]

Since this decision concerning class action would have wide application and would create many complex problems in the diverse school areas of the states concerned, the Court restored the cases

71 347 U.S. at 493.
72 *Ibid.* at 494.
73 347 U.S. at 495 (1953).

to the docket and invited all parties concerned to present rearguments on questions four and five, for formulating decrees to implement its decision. Reargument on the measures and procedures of relief was heard on April 11–14, 1955. The Court announced its opinion and judgments. The judgments of all the lower courts, Delaware expected, were reversed, that of Delaware affirmed. Furthermore, the cases were remanded to the district courts, Delaware excepted:

> . . . to take such proceedings and enter such orders and decrees consistent with this opinion as are necessary and proper to admit to public schools on a racially non-discriminatory basis with all deliberate speed the parties to these cases. During the period of transition the Courts will retain jurisdiction on these cases.[74]

Before announcing this decision the Court knew that "substantial progress" had been made in eliminating racial discrimination in the public schools of the District of Columbia, Kansas, and Delaware but it was also well aware that many states would not react kindly to its final decision. It therefore thought it necessary to add a word of warning. The Court said:

> To effectuate [the interest of the plaintiffs] may call for elimination of a variety of obstacles in making the transition to school systems operated in accordance with the constitutional principles set forth in our May 17, 1954 decision. . . . But it should go without saying that the vitality of these constitutional principles cannot be allowed to yield simply because of disagreement with them.[75]

Furthermore, although the district courts were to retain jurisdiction in each case, the Supreme Court placed upon each state concerned the full burden of a prompt and reasonable start toward full compliance with its May 17, 1954, ruling.

The decision in the Brown case had been acclaimed as presaging a new era for the colored race. It has been accepted as the American fulfillment of the Declaration of Independence for a race which has too long felt the bonds of intellectual captivity. The decision has also been denounced as a blatant judicial usurpation of state powers.

[74] 349 U.S. at 301.
[75] Ibid. at 300.

However, even in the midst of these conflicting opinions the meaning of the Court's decision should not be left in doubt.

The Court did not order either desegregation or integration of the races. It merely held that compulsory segregation solely on the basis of color or race was in itself an unconstitutional discrimination and, consequently, a violation of the equal protection guaranteed by the Fourteenth Amendment.

A cursory review of the seven years which have elapsed since the Brown decision in 1954 reveals certain factors of considerable sociological and political significance. To the credit of the American democratic temperament no large-scale race riots have reddened the pages of our recent history. Even the "massive resistance" of Virginia is gone, although the deep South is still not willing to accept any public school integration. It has resisted every movement toward integration. This resistance ranges from the ineffective nullification and interposition legislation of 1956 and the "Southern Manifesto" of the ninety-six United States Congressmen, who declared the Court's decision a "substitution of naked power for established law" to many diverse and positive measures, legal, economic, and social, aimed at frustrating the Court's decision, such as laws authorizing governors to refuse financial aid to or close any public school which integrated, allowing them to establish grants for attendance at "private schools" and authorizing state educational authorities to establish intricate and evasive systems of "pupil placement."

The year 1957 witnessed the open defiance of Little Rock which evoked Eisenhower's orders sending federal troops into a sovereign state to protect the rights of Negro children. The same year was also the one in which Congress for the first time since 1875 passed a Civil Rights law. The spring of 1960 witnessed two new developments in the Negro struggle for freedom. Congress passed another Civil Rights law protecting the Negroes' right to vote and the deep South was confronted by the lunch-counter "sit-ins" which proved to be at least a moral victory for the Negro even though it came very close to igniting a racial fuse. In May of 1961 a new technique was created and employed by the active forces for integration. The new technique has been called the "Freedom Riders." These riders are a group of Negroes and whites, traveling on interstate buses, who insist on eating together at the bus terminals in the deep South. The first two well heralded rides to Alabama almost triggered a full-scale race riot. One bus was destroyed by fire, several Negroes and white sympathizers were badly beaten and at Montgomery a raging southern mob threatened the very existence of a church and fifteen hundred Negroes gathered there to protest against the Southern segregationists. In response to this open violence and the consequent failure of state authority to preserve law and order, the Attorney General of the United States intervened by sending into Alabama several hundred federal officers. During the past seven years the Court, although subject to bitter criticism even from high places, has continued to whittle away at segregation in education, public parks, bathing beaches, amusement centers, and in the field of transportation. Its progress has been slow but it has been steady. Its attritional effects cannot be minimized. Even in Little Rock Negro students have been admitted into white schools. Defiant and evasive tactics of the states may continue for many years and more serious difficulties may emerge, but it cannot be denied that the Brown decision in 1954 has opened new vistas in our struggle for freedom under law and has enshrined for all to see Harlan's motto of 1896, "the constitution is color blind."

Biracial Public School Education in the South

JOHN W. DONOHUE

Since Monday morning, May 17, 1954, the issue of racial segregation in public education has surely been one of the most publicized in our national life. Because a moral question lies at its heart its impact has been peculiarly profound, striking off a thousand particular incidents, some of them encouraging and some not. If these fragments could be neatly assembled and correlated, perhaps a partial coherency and some ground for cautious generalization might emerge. At the moment, however, comment would be risky and prophecy foolhardy.

For the casual reader of the news, the mention of segregation is likely to invoke a nightmare world streaked by lurid glimpses of violence, fear, and paradox. It is a world inhabited by figures whose names often strike the Northerner as rather exotic: Virgil T. Blossom, Orval Faubus, Autherine Lucy, Minnie Jean Brown, Leander Perez, Omer and Oliver Cromwell Carmichael. The scenes in which they are involved shift from Tuscaloosa to Louisville to Little Rock to New Orleans and are frequently punctuated by a brutal chorus of unreason: "the inebriated fraternity men," as officials of the University of Alabama described them, chanting in the night, "Hey, ho, ho, Autherine must go"; the raucous women in New Orleans hurling vulgarities and shouts of "Communist!" after a priest walking with a white minister and the latter's child to an integrated school; the mob in Little Rock applauding its delegate, a white matron who had gone into the handsome Central High School there to see whether nine Negroes were at class with the nineteen hundred white students and returned to report elegantly over the public address system: "There was no niggers there."

In September, 1957, one read of the Jewish woman in Little Rock who said that its atmosphere reminded her of the Hitlerian Germany she had fled years before. Or one read of the advertisement in the *Arkansas Democrat* summoning all who were against "race mixing" to a rally and signed, "The Group of Patriotic Christians." There was the account of a sixteen-year-old boy lounging in a grocery store in Clinton. "I quit school," he explained. "Maybe you could go to school and look at them. I just couldn't stand being near them. The only reason I went to school last year was so I could kick up something with them." And up on the hill behind the high school a Negro woman waiting on the stoop of her unpainted frame house for her son to come home, was saying: "I've backed up all I'm going to back up. My boy's going to that school and he's going to keep going to that school until he graduates or they kill him. And if they want to fight, I'm ready."[1] There was the account of a famous Negro entertainer who had been asked to make a good-will tour of the Soviet Union but told reporters: "The way they are treating my people in the South, the government can go to hell." There were the pictures from Nashville of some first-graders wearing buttons which read, "Keep schools white" and of a balding segregationist picketing the buildings with a placard in one hand and a Bible in the other.

These sensational vistas, however, need to be placed alongside others which are quieter but more hopeful and perhaps more signifi-

[1] *The New York Times*, Sept. 8, 1957, p. 56.

cant for the future. David Loth and Harold Fleming collected, in *Integration North and South*, a mass of factual evidence justifying the subtitle, "Progress Memorandum." For here are hundreds of instances, many of them small enough, it is true, of integration quietly proceeding in both North and South, not only in education but in private and public employment, housing, recreation, transportation, and community facilities. Nevertheless, the story of segregation in these years following upon the decree of 1954 is still too immediate, too vast and intricate for definitive interpretation even were one to have a detailed, firsthand knowledge of all the factors involved. There is a melancholy lesson to be learned by turning back to certain comments made the day of the decision itself by well known historians and sociologists, north and south. "The decision will be accepted philosophically by many elements of the South in the immediate present," said Arthur M. Schlesinger, Sr. The late Charles S. Johnson, distinguished Negro sociologist and president of Fisk thought "most of the South is ready for it." Howard W. Odum, best known of the white Southern sociologists, agreed: "The South is likely to surprise itself and the nation and do an excellent job of readjustment. We might want to delay a little, so we could get ready. In my opinion, the South for the most part will take it in its stride."[2] On the other hand, perhaps the deeply pessimistic analyses of recent years are also wide of the mark. It may be, as some thoughtful observers have felt, that a negative movement like the present opposition even to token integration must eventually blow itself out.[3]

At any rate, since the current picture is certainly passion-ridden and opaque it will be wiser to concentrate here on certain aspects of the biracial public school question as these appeared prior to May 17, 1954, with the hope that discussion of this sort will provide some illumination. In that year there were in the continental United States some 162 million people of whom about 10 per cent were members

[2] *The New York Times*, May 18, 1954, p. 17.

[3] For varying degrees of pessimism, either on the part of the writers themselves or on the part of those whose opinions they report, see: Wilma Dykeman and James Stokely, "Integration: Third and Critical Phase," *New York Times Magazine*, Nov. 27, 1960, pp. 24, 111–113; Samuel Lubell, "Racial War in the South," *Commentary*, 24 (1957), 113–118; John Bartlow Martin, *The Deep South Says "Never"* (New York: Ballantine Books, 1957), and Stephen P. Ryan, "Climate of the South," *America*, 97 (June 15, 1957), 322–324. This last commentator in a subsequent article spoke somewhat more hopefully, "The South in Retrospect," *America*, 104 (Dec. 3, 1960), 345–347.

of the Negro community. More than 50 millions of all these Americans, nearly a third of the nation, lived in those sixteen states which taken collectively are called by the United States Bureau of the Census the Southern Region. At that moment those states, together with Missouri and the District of Columbia, maintained by law a compulsory bi-racial public school system and in many instances forbade integration in independent schools as well. Three of the sixteen states were not much more than nominally Southern: Delaware, Maryland, and Okla-homa. Eight others had something of the character of border states or at least were not then wholly inflexible in their segregationist senti-ment. Virginia and Florida may perhaps be included here along with West Virginia, North Carolina, Arkansas, Tennessee, Kentucky, and Texas. The remainder was made up of Louisiana, Alabama, South Carolina, Georgia, and Mississippi—the last four constituting the "deep South."[4] Four years earlier the 1950 Census had found that

    [4] For various estimates of both the general and the school populations in the nation as a whole and in the South particularly, handy references are: U.S. Bureau of the Census, *Statistical Abstracts of the United States: 1955* (Seventy-sixth Edition), (Washington, D.C.: Government Printing Office, 1955); Rose Marie Smith and W. Vance Grant, *Statistical Summary of Education 1953–1954,* U.S. Department of Health, Education and Welfare (Washington, D.C.: Govern-ment Printing Office, 1957); Carol Joy Hobson, *Statistics of Public Elementary and Secondary Education of Negroes in the Southern States: 1951–1952,* Circular No. 444: U.S. Department of Health, Education and Welfare (Washington, D.C.: Government Printing Office, 1955). More specialized statistical studies of specific phases of Southern education are found in: Truman M. Pierce *et al., White and Negro Schools in the South: An Analysis of Biracial Education* (Englewood Cliffs, N.J.: Prentice-Hall, 1955). This is the report of one of the large-scale studies carried on in 1953–1954 by the so-called "Ashmore project" underwritten by the Fund for the Advancement of Education, which engaged some forty-five re-searchers in a comprehensive survey of the Southern school scene.
    The limits of the South are variously estimated. The United States Bureau of the Census divides the Southern Region into South Atlantic States (Delaware, Maryland, Virginia, West Virginia, North and South Carolina, Georgia, Florida, and the District of Columbia); East South Central (Kentucky, Tennessee, Ala-bama, Mississippi) and West South Central (Arkansas, Louisiana, Oklahoma, and Texas). Students of the segregation issues have sometimes found it helpful to speak of the states as "nominally border" (e.g., Maryland); "genuinely border" (e.g., Kentucky, West Virginia); "less rigidly segregationist" (e.g., Florida, Virginia) and the "Deep South." Pierce and his associates limited their study, cited above, to thirteen states, *viz.,* Alabama, Arkansas, Florida, Georgia, Ken-tucky, Louisiana, Mississippi, North Carolina, Oklahoma, South Carolina, Ten-nessee, Texas and Virginia. For the South as thus defined they give the following percentages: In 1900, 34.3 per cent of the total population of this region was Negro; in 1950 it had declined to 22.5 per cent. See Pierce *et al., op. cit.,* p. 117.

ten and a half million Negroes, or 70 per cent of all the Negroes in the United States, were living in the South. By 1954 this percentage was probably somewhat diminished since the pronounced trend of Negro migration to other regions had continued during the intervening years. That migration had already reduced the Negro minority in the Southern states from more than a third of the total population in 1900 to about a fifth in 1950. In no one of these states, moreover, were Negroes in the majority. In nine of them, one out of every five persons was accounted a Negro in 1950 while the Negro percentage of the total state population ranged, throughout the region as a whole, from a low of 6.5 per cent in Oklahoma to a high of 45.2 per cent in Mississippi.

Within this rudimentary framework the broad numerical lines of the school picture may be inscribed. In May, 1954, better than one out of every five of those 162 million Americans was somewhere in school —somewhere, as a full or part-time student, along the ascending rungs of the two educational ladders, the public and independent systems, each of which mounts from nursery class to graduate seminar. Of these 36 million students, nearly 29 million were enrolled in public elementary and secondary schools, about three quarters of them in the grades from kindergarten to Grade 8; the rest in high school.

But in seventeen states, these public school children were systematically distributed into a biracial structure. Nearly 9 million of them were in separate white schools with white teachers while over 2½ million were in separate Negro schools staffed by almost 80,000 Negro teachers and principals. The school population patterns showed, of course, the same sort of variation from state to state as did those of the general population. Where Delaware had not quite 10,000 children in its Negro schools, Georgia, Mississippi, and North Carolina each had more than a quarter of a million. In Mississippi, Negro children of school age (5–17) actually constituted 50.9 per cent of all the state's children in that age group in 1950. This was because a higher birth rate and a higher mortality rate made the Negro community a "younger" one than the white. It may be noted, finally, that in 1953–1954 there were some 60,000 school districts in the United States. Although the seventeen states maintaining compulsorily segregated schools were educating a third of the children in the nation, they accounted for only about 10 to 14 per cent of all these school districts since the district in the South was often coterminous with the county unit and therefore quite large. More than half of those Southern school districts, however, would be unaffected by the decision of May 17, 1954, since they did not include children of both races.[5]

The legal, as distinguished from the philosophical, rationale of this system of biracial public education had developed over a century. In 1849 the Massachusetts State Supreme Court upheld the refusal of the Boston School Committee to admit Sarah Roberts to a white school nearer her home than the one provided for Negroes. Six years later the Massachusetts legislature abolished Jim Crow schooling altogether, but in *Roberts* v. *City of Boston* the State Supreme Court ruled that segregation of the races did not, of itself, constitute discrimination. What then would? For one thing, allocation of inferior facilities to either race. In recent decades, responsible Southern leaders have tacitly conceded that unequal facilities are proof of an injustice in the civil order for they have not mounted any programmatic defense of the cruel inequalities which biracial education has actually involved for the Negro minority. They have relied rather on the doctrine which the U.S. Supreme Court borrowed from *Roberts* and enunciated in *Plessy* v. *Ferguson* in 1896. In the latter decision the Court, settling a dispute over segregation in railway carriages, illustrated its thesis that separate but equal facilities imply no violation of constitutionally guaranteed rights by a somewhat gratuitous reference to segregated schools as proof of this proposition. On the morning of Monday, May 17, 1954, the same U.S. Supreme Court, numbering among its members several Southerners, unanimously overturned this earlier doctrine by concluding that segregation of the races, at least as currently practiced, does indeed constitute discrimination and that "separate educational facilities are inherently unequal."[6]

THE HISTORICAL RECORD

Our concern here is indeed with segregation—or as the expressive South African term puts it so chillingly, *apartheid,* apartness, the very

[5] Don Shoemaker (ed.), *With All Deliberate Speed: Segregation-Desegregation in Southern Schools* (New York: Harper & Brothers, 1957), p. 202. Toward the close of 1960 it was reported that 2,834 Southern school districts were still biracial and that only 768 of these had any sort of integration so that a mere 6 per cent of the Negro children involved were actually in integrated schools. See Dykeman and Stokely, *op. cit.,* p. 24.
[6] *Brown* v. *Board of Education of Topeka et al.,* 347 U.S. 495 (1954).

opposite of atonement—but segregation of one particular sort, segregation in the public elementary and secondary schools. This type of segregation may be described as the separation of white children from Negro children in the affairs of formal education on the sole, or at least decisive, basis of race and this by mandate of specific statute. The student of educational matters may ask two questions about such a situation. First, what have been its general characteristics as a historical phenomenon? Secondly, what quasi philosophy of education has the dominant and segregating majority entertained as the ideological basis of the biracial school system?

A rapid overview of Southern educational history since the Civil War leaves one with three impressions. It is clear in the first place that when the Supreme Court rejected the concept of separate but equal facilities it was rejecting a juristic projection, not an educational reality. Indeed, one reason why Negro leaders have attacked the idea of a biracial school system is that inferior facilities for Negroes seem to be its inevitable consequence. A thoroughly itemized comparison of the two sets of schools in the South is very hard to construct, as all those who have tried it remark, because educational practices vary from state to state throughout the region and certain data are not easily come by. But after all, a highly detailed study is scarcely necessary, for as one research team has observed: "Even simple observation has always been enough to show that Negro schools have in general been inferior to white schools."[7] This despite the fact that in the late 1950's some states were taking hurry-up steps to "equalize."

Still, the story of Negro education in the South from 1865 to 1954 offers some ground for cautious optimism about the future. It has not been a history of an unbroken and steady ascent toward equality but rather one of tormented and erratic advance. Nevertheless, it has added up in the final reckoning to a record of progress—of progress from violent denial of any schooling for Negroes, to a reluctant concession of minimal schooling, and finally to some concern for facilities and staffs increasingly more adequate. Was it the moral pressure of the national commitment to the ideal of equality that brought this about? Perhaps. And perhaps Myrdal was right when he commented that the Southern whites' caste policy, always half-hearted, was par-

[7] Pierce *et al., op. cit.,* p. v.

ticularly so in education because these Southerners were also good Americans with the "standardized American ideals about education."[8]

Finally, the historic record suggests very strongly that, quite apart from its ethical validity, the whole concept of "separate but equal" is self-dissolving. For the more nearly equal the white and Negro schools become at the literal level of personnel and equipment, the more radically unequal the whole system is likely to seem to the Negro people. As they are progressively better educated, their status as second-class citizens, a status harshly symbolized, enforced, and embodied by biracialism in schooling, transportation, housing, and recreation, is bound to become ever more galling. It is, after all, not a system freely chosen by each of the two groups—something which the Christian would regard as bad enough—but a system imposed by one upon the other and made possible only by more or less disenfranchising the minority. Besides, it is hard enough to make two schoolhouses perfectly equal, even as to their sites, and it is impossible to make all the seats in a bus or theater equally desirable.

Any consideration of public education in the South must begin by recalling that the public school ideal as we know it today, with its special reverence for equality of opportunity and for freedom, together with its special shyness of the religious base of these values, was not a Southern creation and perhaps never fully marshaled the convictions of the white South behind it. At least, the existence of the segregated school suggests as much. In Colonial times there was an ideological division in educational philosophy between the aristocratic, rural, feudal culture of the tobacco South and the high-minded biblical commonwealths of New England. Where the celebrated Massachusetts "Ould Deluder" Act of 1647 called for the universal instruction of youth so that all, by reading the Scriptures, might outmaneuver Satan and find salvation, and hence required every township of fifty householders to appoint a teacher of reading and writing, the Virginia colony left it to individual families to do what they liked. Historians have often remarked the further division between the North and South at the time of the American Revolution, for logically

---

[8] Gunnar Myrdal *et al.*, *An American Dilemma: The Negro Problem and Modern Democracy* (New York: Harper & Brothers, 1944), p. 896. The South, to be sure, has given its own nuances to these "standardized ideals."

the South could not wholly go along with the idealism of equality reflected in the Declaration of Independence and the Constitution.

During the nineteenth century it was always New England which took the lead in conceiving and executing the successive measures which built up the public school structure: tax-support at first allowed and then required; the institution of free schools reinforced by compulsory education laws; the development and dissemination of the high school idea; the progressive secularization of publicly maintained institutions. In all these matters the South followed, but slowly —partly because these steps were alien to the spirit of the plantation world and the small backwoods farms; partly because of the destructive effects of the Civil War; and partly, too, because it had never quite subscribed to the philosophy making these developments dynamic. The history of compulsory education laws is a good case in point. Before the Civil War the only state to have such a law was Massachusetts, but by 1883 they were in force in all of the New England and some of the Middle Atlantic, Central, and far western states. As late as 1914, however, six Southern states—Alabama, Florida, Georgia, Mississippi, South Carolina, and Texas—still had no such statutes. Even where they were passed, during the following years, their requirements were stingy enough. The first compulsory education legislation in Mississippi straggled along in 1918 and called for school attendance by children from seven to fourteen for sixty days annually, or for forty if this were all the local school board could bring itself to furnish. Moreover, this regulation itself was left to the option of the individual counties and some form of such option continued for at least another decade. This does not mean, of course, that all Mississippi schools had so abbreviated a term, but it does reveal the legal mechanism that made it possible to consign to Negro schools the scantiest of rations, a meager diet of educational grits.

Given this background, one is not surprised to find that attorneys for Virginia in the school cases told the Supreme Court:

We point out that the question is, nevertheless, not a simple one of whether schools shall be segregated or not. There is the further alternative of whether there shall be schools or not. We find nothing in the Constitution that requires public education by any state. Again, this is not a threat; it is a simple statement of fact. Georgia, for example, has appropriated more than 100 million dollars in 1953 for the public schools. The appropriation is conditioned on continued segregation. If segregation ends, so do State funds for the public schools.[9]

If the South was slow to provide even for the public education of white children it is not remarkable that the history of its Negro schools departs so sharply from the usual patterns of American educational idealism. So long as slavery was established, the formal education of Negroes was generally forbidden, although individual planters could do what they wished and the laws were, in fact, often ignored for the sake of training up cultivated house servants. It was also possible for freedmen in both the North and the South to acquire some learning, at least by setting up their own schools. When the Civil War ended, there were in the South approximately 27 million whites, 4 million Negroes who had been slaves in 1860 and some 400,000 who had been freedmen at that time. The South in those days had practically no public school system of any sort. From a situation of near chaos one might well wonder what would emerge for the education of the bewildered, recently emancipated Negro—who would provide; what the attitude of the white Southerner would be and what sort of historic course the Negro school would traverse.

The first efforts to educate the new Negro freedman, as well as most subsequent measures for the improvement of Negro education, were not Southern in inspiration at all, much less publicly supported.[10] In roughly chronological succession, the promoters of Negro *public* education in the past nine decades have been Northern Protestant missionaries, the federal government (for instance, through the "Bureau for Freedmen, Refugees and Abandoned Lands," from 1865 to 1870), the Southern Negro community, Northern philanthropists, and the Southern state and local governments themselves.

As early as 1861 the American Missionary Association was caring for the "contrabands of war," as refugees from neighboring planta-

[9] In the Supreme Court of the United States, October Term, 1953, Brief for Appellees in No. 4 (*Davis* v. *County School Board*) on Reargument (Nov. 30, 1954), p. 36. In an earlier brief, under date of October 9, 1952, the attorneys for Virginia pointed out that the public school system in their state dated only from about 1870 and had developed so slowly that as late as 1920 there were only 31,000 children in the Virginia public schools.

[10] This is the judgment of Southern educators themselves. See Pierce *et al.*, *op. cit.*, p. 79: ". . . the general apathy toward Negro education has been such that, almost without exception advances have come about through the influence of forces from outside the South."

tions were called, in a little schoolhouse at Hampton, Virginia. Schools of this sort were set up in other parts of the South and staffed by teachers whom the missionary societies supported. These people were often motivated by a noble religious idealism companioned, at times, by a proselytizing spirit. When George W. Cable was still working in his native New Orleans in the 1870's he combated a proposal to make religious training compulsory in the public schools. Cable was himself a devout Protestant and a severe critic of Southern racism, so his opposition to this project as an instance of Northern oppression was due neither to impiety nor unreconstructed prejudice. He simply thought it unfair to Catholics and Jews, and this suggests that the actual aim of the proposal was to make the public schools Protestant in tone.[11]

Admirable as the early work of Northern teachers was, it still encountered two discouraging obstacles. For one thing, the physical facilities in those first Negro schools were often wretched. A woman employed in Louisiana by the Friends Association for the Aid and Elevation of the Freedmen, wrote in April of 1863:

I opened school here in a rough log house, thirty feet square and so open that the crevices admitted light sufficient without the aid of windows. The furniture consisted of undressed plank benches without backs, from ten to twelve feet long, and in the center of the room stood an old steam-boat stove about four feet long which had been taken out of the river.

Even this was better than the situation of another teacher in the same area who lived on "strong pork and sour bread" and taught in a floorless, windowless shed.[12]

A good many of these miseries, of course, may be reasonably ascribed to the shattering conditions created by war. But the second, and more significant block thrown in the way of the white teachers from the North had even uglier and less impersonal origins. For the racist temper which convulses segregationists today was paralleled in the 1860's by fierce opposition to the notion of any schooling at all for Negroes. At best the white Southerner dismissed such projects

[11] Arlin Turner, *George W. Cable: A Biography* (Durham: Duke University Press, 1956), p. 41.
[12] Bell Irvin Wiley, *Southern Negroes: 1861–1865* (New Haven: Yale University Press, 1938), p. 271. The edition quoted here is a reissue by Rinehart in 1953.

scornfully but often enough the teachers, whose pay was frequently in arrears, were unable to hire lodgings, were denied credit at the stores, and saw their pupils stoned and the ramshackle schoolhouses burned or defaced.[13] This hostility toward the idea of education for Negroes gave ground slowly and has by no means retired from the field even yet. It is epitomized and partly explained by the remark of a sawmill owner in North Carolina who in 1901 said that he found "the uneducated negro to be the best we have for drudgery."[14]

The five-year tenure of the Freedmen's Bureau meant some improvement in these conditions and a constructive period for Negro education. During the years 1865 to 1870 the Bureau coordinated federal and private efforts, helped in the founding of such distinguished centers of Negro higher education as Fisk, Atlanta, and Howard universities, and set up 4,239 lower schools staffed by 9,307 teachers of 247,333 pupils. Obviously most of these must have been one- or two-teacher schools. Indeed, even as late as the 1940's, 82 per cent of the Negro elementary schools in eight Southern states (Alabama, Arkansas, Delaware, Louisiana, Maryland, Mississippi, South Carolina, and Virginia) were still of this sort.[15] In any agricultural society, of course, the small school is almost inevitable, for the central consolidated institution is not particularly feasible for very young children, and until the quite recent process of urbanization the South has been decidedly rural. Even today some two-fifths of its land area is in forests, for the shift to an industrial economy gathered speed only after 1940. Granted this, it is still true that the ungraded classroom, the little wooden building set in a dusty yard along a country road, is an imperfect sort of educational setting.

When in 1870 the South began to regain management of its own affairs it found that the Reconstruction legislatures, so lately moved out, had left the states, among other legacies, their first sketchy

[13] *Ibid.*, pp. 273–275.

[14] Quoted in Louis R. Harlan, *Separate and Unequal: Public School Campaigns and Racism in the Southern Seaboard States 1901–1915* (Chapel Hill: University of North Carolina Press, 1958), p. 102.

[15] E. Franklin Frazier, *The Negro in the United States* (New York: The Macmillan Company, 1949), p. 437, note 3. In 1951–1952, writes an education statistician, 1-, 2- and 3-teacher "schools represented 70 percent of all Negro schools in the Southern States, as compared with less than half of the total in white schools." Hobson, *op. cit.*, p. 4. For a brief, nontechnical résumé of the Southern economy see Pierce *et al.*, *op. cit.*, pp. 119–122.

systems of universal public education. From one point of view, the reaction of the restored governments was commendable. They not only accepted this innovation but for a while even maintained the white and Negro schools on a basis more or less equal—equally scant. In Mississippi, for instance, white and Negro teachers were receiving the same salaries into the early 1880's.[16] On the other hand, an unmistakable reluctance hobbled the whole evolution of Negro education. For one thing, although only two of the Southern states, Arkansas and Florida, had a statutory provision for a segregated public school system at the time they ratified the Fourteenth Amendment, within a year after ratification five more had made such an enactment and the rest followed suit shortly. In early years the support of Negro schools was sometimes limited to those revenues derived from taxes paid by Negroes—obviously a slender resource considering the Negroes' impoverished status. Scattered attempts to conduct integrated schools in Louisiana and South Carolina were heatedly overcome. Moreover, there was a general disposition to confine Negro education to rudiments and nonspecialized vocational training. These attitudes appear to have been shaped by a racist doctrine in which the central thesis was the conviction that since the Negro was by his very nature inferior, biracialism in education was strictly necessary. Consequently, about the best face the white Southerner could put upon the new civic order was a rather defeatist one. "The great question now to be solved," said Governor David S. Walker of Florida in 1867 to a meeting of emancipated Negroes, "is whether two different races can live in peace together under the same government with equal political rights. In my reading of history, I do not remember any instance in which this has ever been done. But God has placed the work upon us and with His blessing we must try our best to accomplish it."[17] The Knights of the White Camellia, of course, were not so resigned.

At any rate, in the 1890's when the demands and the power of the

[16] Horace M. Bond, *The Education of the Negro in the American Social Order* (New York: Prentice-Hall, 1934), pp. 96–97.

[17] Semiweekly *Floridan,* Tallahassee, April 23, 1867, p. 2, quoted in Richard W. Ervin, Attorney General of the State of Florida, and Ralph E. Odum, Assistant Attorney General, State of Florida, Amicus Curiae *Brief of the Attorney General of Florida,* in the Supreme Court of the United States, October Term, 1954 (no date or number), p. 95.

"poor whites" were growing through the medium of the Populist movement, the whole civic and educational position of the Southern Negro sharply deteriorated. Tax support for Negro schools was restricted and funds were diverted to white institutions. This trend continued for several decades. In 1912, for instance, the Southern states were spending less than $3.00 in teachers' salaries for each Negro child to every $10.32 for each white child.[18] Corresponding inequalities marked every other phase of current expenditure as well as capital outlay. During those years the South was struggling to improve public education all along the line. As late as 1908 there were only two four-year public high schools in North Carolina and North Carolina was a relatively advanced state. Under the impetus provided by a private association, the Southern Education Board, which was a charitable partnership of Northern philanthropists and Southern educators, this state had raised the number of its high schools to 89 by 1915.

Yet this record of progress had its dismal side for that improvement of educational facilities for white children did not mean a parallel improvement of Negro schools. In *Separate and Unequal* Louis R. Harlan has shown, by piecing together a multitude of facts, that the white schools were often strengthened at the expense of the Negro ones. For when Negro children were counted in for the purposes of tax levies and all but counted out in the distribution of the monies raised, the biracial school system was making possible a nicely economical expansion of the white resources. Thus in South Carolina in 1915 the Negro children represented 61.02 per cent of the total school population but their schools received only 11.24 per cent of the school funds. When the cases decided in 1954 were being argued in the courts, it was sometimes said by Southern attorneys general that the white people of the states in question so prized the biracial

[18] Frazier, *op. cit.*, p. 427. Frazier brings together here various statistics indicating how poorly supported the Negro schools were and how limited was the amount of education obtained by Negro children prior to World War I. There were in 1912, for instance, only 64 public high schools for Negroes and the majority of these were in border states. Of course, this picture has changed dramatically in recent years. Thus Hobson gives figures showing that whereas the 17 states with biracial school systems had 33,341 pupils in the Negro secondary schools in 1919–1920, they had 372,362 in 1951–1952, Hobson, *op. cit.*, p. 7.

school system as to be willing to bear the heavy cost of its support. Actually, as the cited study shows, for a good part of its history the system saved the white taxpayer money.[19]

Nevertheless, the upward climb of the Negro school though retarded was not halted. Credit for this is owing in large measure to a rather unusual factor in the history of American public education, namely, to the supporting role played by private Northern philanthropy. This stimulation and aid compensated in some measure for the negligence of the Southern localities and kept Negro education on its road of painfully slow advance. From the 1860's until its dissolution in 1914, the Peabody Fund made contributions toward the support of Negro common schools and higher education. In the 1880's the Slater Fund joined the work, and in 1905 Anna T. Jeanes, a Philadelphia Quakeress, made the gift which established the Jeanes teachers. These were supervisors skilled in industrial education who traveled about among the rural schools and helped organize classes in domestic science, gardening, and crafts. By 1929 there were over 300 of such experts and a third of their maintenance came from the Jeanes Fund, the rest from public resources.

The General Education Board, supported by Rockefeller gifts, underwrote a variety of projects including the salaries of white state supervisors who served without official authority under the state superintendents. Most spectacular of all these philanthropies was that of the Julius Rosenwald Fund which between 1913 and its founder's death in 1932 built 5,358 schools in 883 counties of 15 Southern states at a cost of nearly $28,500,000. The Rosenwald Fund provided 15 per cent of this sum; gifts of Negroes themselves accounted for another 17 per cent; local white benefactors contributed 4 per cent and the remainder, 64 per cent, came from the public tax funds of the Southern states concerned.[20] It has sometimes been said that this Northern charity dulled the Southern sense of civic responsibility for Negro education. But as Frazier points out in connection with these figures on the work of the Rosenwald Fund, in some instances the

[19] Harlan, *op. cit., passim,* but especially pp. 9–32, 249–257 and for the comparison of South Carolina's expenditures for white and Negro schools, p. 15, note 33.

[20] Frazier, *op. cit.,* p. 429.

stimulus of the Foundations' activity quickened both the Negro community and the official Southern conscience.

Nevertheless, it seems to have been generally true that, until the post-World War II years, Southern localities, far from feeling any obligation to provide equal facilities, were with difficulty brought to feel much obligation at all. Thus it could happen that even relatively poor private agencies were able to provide more effective schooling in rural areas of the deep South than public facilities afforded. In 1929, for instance, the Reverend Thomas McNamara, S.S.J., a Roman Catholic priest of the Josephite congregation, was sent to St. Augustine's Parish, New Roads, Louisiana. At that time the state supplied only the most sketchy sort of elementary education for Negro children. A traveling teacher conducted classes for a few months in any handy vacant barn or shed. In September, 1933, Father McNamara was finally able to open a full-term eight-grade school with 130 children and four lay teachers. But the indignation of the local white residents, which had delayed his project in the first place on the grounds that field hands had no need of so extended a training, continued to harass the work, and the pastor was unable to obtain bus transportation for those of his pupils who lived at a distance.[21]

During the depression years, when the South was, in a famous presidential phrase, the nation's No. 1 economic problem, a curiously ambivalent situation developed. So far as surface aspects went, the position of Negro schools seemed threatened anew. The entire nation was in the grip of economic pressure, but the squeeze was worst in the South. Schools everywhere found their funds diminishing if not dried up but the drought in the South was extreme. At the same time the demands made upon these schools were heavier than ever. On the eve of the depression, Negroes had for the first time been going to school in the same proportion as whites although their academic terms were shorter and they put in fewer of them.[22] Now with jobs unavailable, school enrollments shot up though revenues, of course, did not. A few of the dreary statistics are emblematic. In 1935–1936, the minimum

[21] George J. Turner, "The Josephites and Catholic Education in the United States," (Unpublished Ph.D. Dissertation, Department of Education, Fordham University, 1957), pp. 159–160.

[22] Harry S. Ashmore, *The Negro and the Schools* (Chapel Hill: The University of North Carolina Press, 1954), p. 26.

annual salary of a Negro teacher in Georgia was $282. During the thirties current operating expenditures per pupil amounted to $45 in the South, or less than one-half what they were in the nation as a whole.

Nevertheless, these bleak years were marked by certain significant ethical developments. Harry S. Ashmore, summing up the findings of a number of researchers, points out that it was in the depression decade that white Southern leaders became more sensitive to their responsibilities toward Negro education and even started to take quite seriously the second adjective in the "separate but equal" slogan. At the same time, Negro leadership itself matured, particularly in the North, and its strategy in the field of education began to take shape in the mid-1930's when the biracial structure was first challenged. In 1935 the Maryland Court of Appeals ruled that Donald Murray, a Negro, had to be admitted to the University of Maryland Law School since all other arrangements would have been "unequal." Three years later Murray was graduated from this school, twelfth in a class of thirty-seven.

These subtle shifts in the prevailing climate of opinion became still more marked with the return of prosperity, especially in the years after World War II. There was a resumption of the pattern of material progress in public education in the sense of an increase in enrollments, revenues, personnel, and facilities and although the South still lagged some steps behind the rest of the nation, it was narrowing the gap. In 1940 education in the thirteen states studied by Pierce and his associates received 27.9 per cent of all state revenues; in 1952, 34.7 per cent. In 1940 there were no Negroes on the school boards of any of those states save Oklahoma, but in 1953 seven of the states had Negro members on local school boards, generally urban ones, and Kentucky and North Carolina had a Negro on their state boards.[23]

It is, of course, true that during the decade 1940–1950 enrollments actually declined because of the low birth rates of the depression years and, so far as the Negro schools were concerned, because of the migrations from the South. But in other respects there were important gains. For instance, in the period from 1919–1920 to 1951–1952, high

[23] Pierce *et al., op. cit.,* pp. 80, 149.

school enrollment in the country as a whole doubled but in the Negro school system of the South it increased ninefold. In the latter year the graduates of Negro high schools represented an increase of 66 per cent over the number in 1939–1940. The average length of term in Negro schools in 1919–1920 was 119 days. In 1951–1952 it was 176. In 1951–1952, moreover, the length of the term was practically the same in Negro as in white schools and the discrepancy between the average annual salaries of members of the instructional staffs of white and Negro schools was substantially reduced.[24] Many of the Southern states also embarked in the early fifties upon an impressive program of expenditures for capital outlay: new sites, buildings, equipment. In 1953–1954, to cite one example, South Carolina allocated $93 millions for school building funds and $62 millions of these went for Negro schools. It must be recalled, however, that there were decades of neglect to make up. For even in the year of the Brown decision, the South's annual expenditure for each of its school children, based on average daily attendance, was $161 compared with $225 for the nation as a whole. A careful study by the U.S. Department of Health, Education and Welfare summarized thus the standing of Negro schools in 1952:

In spite of the large sums spent in recent years to improve the Negro school plant, there is still a long way to go before school construction catches up with the need for school housing. One measure of the inadequate facilities characteristic of Negro schools is the value of school property per pupil in average daily attendance. As reported by six Southern States, the amount was $204.98 for Negro schools, as compared with $484.51 in white schools in 1951–52. For the country as a whole, the value of school property per pupil was $600.[25]

On the eve of the Supreme Court decision, then, at least part of the responsible Southern white community was moving toward a literal

[24] Hobson, *op. cit.*, pp. 3–4. In six states the average length of term in Negro schools exceeded that for white schools and in one state the average salary for Negro schools exceeded that for white schools. This survey reports the average annual salary in 1951–1952, per member of the instructional staff of 11 Southern states and the District of Columbia. For Negro schools it was $2,587; for white schools, $2,975. In both instances this was below the average annual salary of $3,801 outside the South.

[25] *Ibid.*, p. 6. *The New York Times* for May 18, 1954, p. 19, reports the 1953–1954 building program in South Carolina.

construing of the doctrine of "separate but equal."[26] Subsequent events have shown that there was no comparable readiness to accept the Negroes' own rejection of that same concept as intrinsically contradictory. The American ethos may have been persuading the white Southerner that Negro educational facilities should be equal, but his regional ideology seems so far to have convinced him that they ought also to be separate. "The Virginia people," said a Brief for the Appellees in *Davis* v. *County School Board*, "overwhelmingly believe that segregated education is proper." And a later brief on behalf of the same state observed: "The question before this Court for decision in this case is the constitutionality of segregation by race in the high schools of Prince Edward County, Virginia. There are no doubt principles involved of a broader application. . . ."[27]

At any rate, there are principles of some sort latent in the Southern ideology and if they are drawn out they may add up to a rudimentary "philosophy of education." To seek for these principles is not so much to inquire into the racial and cultural facts of Southern life and education as into the concepts constructed to intellectualize and interpret those concrete realities. Such a venture in explication is, however, rather risky, so that the following pages must necessarily be tentative.

PHILOSOPHY OF EDUCATION IN AMERICA

Our times have witnessed prodigious industry in writing and research on educational problems. Part of the great mass of books, articles, surveys, reports, theses, bulletins, abstracts, indices, and

[26] Much was made in the segregation cases of this acceptance of the principle of equality. Thus we find in: In the Supreme Court of the United States, October Term, 1953, Brief for Appellees in No. 4 (*Davis* v. *County School Board*) in Reply to Supplemental Brief for the United States on Reargument (December 7, 1953), p. 14, extracts from the Georgia and Virginia statutes of 1870 calling for segregated but equal facilities. It is noted that the wording of the Virginia law of 1870 is almost the same as that of the law in force in 1952.

[27] See: In the Supreme Court of the United States, October Term, 1952, Brief for Appellees in No. 191 (*Davis* v. *County School Board*) (October 9, 1952), p. 9, and: In the Supreme Court of the United States, October Term, 1953, Brief for Appellees in No. 4 (*Davis* v. *County School Board*) on Reargument (November 30, 1953), p. 1.

bibliographies are those works, relatively few, which belong to the flexible category of the philosophy of education. Although the genre has historical antecedents it is, to a great extent, a twentieth-century hybrid like the motel. Contributions to this field are often designed as classroom texts. They make a sustained effort to relate a generalized discussion of the aims, curricula, methods, and agencies of education to a complete philosophy of the real, of life, knowledge, and value. In a day when philosophy in the university world is highly specialized if not absorbed in linguistic problems, this sort of undertaking is a survival of an older enthusiasm for synoptic world views. No doubt the expansion and intricacy of technical philosophical erudition makes these more spacious projects seem comparatively thin. But if philosophies of education rarely engage the strictly philosophical discussion at that level of profundity which the academic philosopher has come to expect, still they do take up many of the crucial questionings and feelings actually preoccupying modern man and perhaps to some extent they compensate in range and relevancy for what they lack in subtlety and depth.

Nowhere has the philosophy of education as a professional discipline been cultivated so assiduously and with such luxuriant results as in the United States. Considering the enormous size and complexity of our school systems and the universal American esteem for education as an instrument of upward social mobility, this is not surprising. A good many competing theories cry their wares in this philosophical market place where one finds representatives of instrumentalism, neorealism, idealism, totalitarian concepts of democracy, and defenders of a Christian Humanism. Each of these tries to provide a conceptual framework for the whole educational enterprise. Since this enterprise is essentially moral in character, concerned as it is with the means and choices that develop a mature and ethical personality, philosophers of education themselves exhibit a pronounced ethical orientation. Very often their chief concern is to articulate the *mystique* of the American Idea, as they understand it, and to sketch the portraits both of the political community which is to nourish that idea and the good citizen who is to embody it.

The moral concern of the various philosophies of education shows itself in devotion to certain Christian ideals of conduct even when their authors themselves do not accept the faith on which Christian morality rests. Chief among these ideals is that of the genuinely rational, democratic community in which friendship flourishes among all the citizens because their true equality, not only within the comparatively delimited perspective of law but also in the ordinary affairs of community living, is not restricted by any legal or social discriminations based on class, race, or religion. This value, itself a somewhat low-pressure version of the commandment of fraternal love, is sometimes poorly expressed. Sometimes it is equated with a naïve egalitarianism or with absolute majoritarian rule. Nevertheless, it is a true value and to give it life and substance would be to incarnate the Christian inspiration in the secular order to no small extent. Anyone who has glanced at contemporary philosophies of education, or indeed any writings on educational administration or methods, knows how pervasive is this notion of "the democratic way of life." It enfolds, with more or less exactness of expression, a concept of full equality quite at variance with that curious concept of legal equality, or classified equality among equals, which was sometimes advanced in the arguments on the segregation cases. In the Brief for the State of Kansas on Reargument in *Brown* v. *Board of Education of Topeka*, for example, it was argued that the 39th Congress in drawing up the Fourteenth Amendment intended to secure for Negroes "the essential incidents of citizenship." This meant, it was said, such fully protected rights as those of personal security (life), liberty, and property. But that concept of basic rights did not include "the right to mingle with other races in the public schools" nor did it require freedom from segregation as its guarantee.[28] The Brief contrasts this icy concept of classified equality sustained by Southerners in the debates of a century ago with the "extremist" demand for absolute equality which Sumner advocated when in 1866 he called upon the Senate to abolish "all laws and customs . . . establishing any oligarchical prejudices and any distinctions of rights on account of color or race."[29]

Nevertheless, the democratic way of life—to say nothing of the

[28] In the Supreme Court of the United States, October Term, 1953, Brief for the State of Kansas in No. 1 (*Brown* v. *Board of Education of Topeka*) on Reargument, n.d., pp. 15, 17–19.

[29] *Ibid.*, p. 18. In the debate about equality an apothegm often cited is this from the Supreme Court in 1896: "A statute which implies merely a legal distinction between the white and colored races . . . has no tendency to destroy the legal equality of the two races." *Plessy* v. *Ferguson*, 163 U.S. 543 (1896).

Christian ethic—is widely understood in American educational theory to imply something very like Sumner's absolute equality rather
than any classified equality. Its specific application to formal schooling is found in the universally applauded principle of equal educational opportunity for all. Thus when the case of *Davis* v. *County
School Board* was being argued before the Federal District Court in
Richmond late in the winter of 1952, Robert L. Carter, counsel for
the plaintiffs, brought forward a number of statements from Virginia's own educational publications which echoed the common
themes of democracy and equality and their implications for education. Questioning Thomas J. McIlwaine, Division Superintendent of
Schools in Prince Edward County, Carter asked: "Do you or don't
you adhere to the belief that one of the major bases of learning is
direct experience from the participation in activities?" McIlwaine
replied that he did adhere to that belief. "And what direct experience
is there of an interracial nature in your school program?" was the
next question. "That has not been brought up in our school program
at all."[30]

It is remarkable, though, that despite their general principles,
American writers on educational theory even up to the mid-1950's
are almost universally silent on the issue of segregation. In some
cases this is because their thought moves within the technical framework of a formal philosophy and does not easily encounter highly
concrete questions unless they have already begun to dominate the
consciousness of society. A great many school administrators, however, also deal from time to time in theoretical statements and they
would be expected to be sensitively aware of and willing to tackle

[30] Quoted in the transcript of evidence from the lower court in: Supreme Court
of the United States, October Term, 1952: Transcript of Record in No. 191
(July 12, 1952), p. 68.
It is hardly surprising, of course, if school officials use the concepts and terms
which are common currency in their profession. It is worth noting, however, that
the remarks of the witness, Mr. McIlwaine, sometimes contained the suggestion
of the kind of qualification the South might expect. Thus when he was asked
about the fundamental objectives of the schools under his care he replied: "Of
course, our fundamental objective is to turn out good citizens, in the first place.
Of course, there is a segment that we do try to prepare for college. There are
others whom we would like to prepare in such a way that they would take their
places in society at the level at which they propose to live and function."—*ibid.,*
p. 62. This may seem unexceptionable enough but in the Southern context the
final sentence is at least ambiguous.

the live issues. But their silence was also practically total, even when they were Northerners working in the North.[31] It is not surprising, therefore, if Southerners overlooked the discrepancy between a biracial educational system and some of the fundamental principles of most American philosophies of education. Such an oversight, besides, is made easier because Southern segregated education has had its own embryonic theory whose key positions are seldom systematically elaborated but are not hard to ascertain.

PHILOSOPHY OF BIRACIAL EDUCATION

This defense of segregation has been voiced in tones ranging from the shrilly venomous to the dryly legal. There are, for instance, the frankly passionate and racialistic appeals whose current archetype is Judge Tom P. Brady's *Black Monday*. There are tracts like Herman E. Talmadge's *You and Segregation* which, though somewhat less violent, still include inflammatory references to intermingling and intermarriage. Finally, there is the measured sort of statement found in the argumentation advanced by lawyers for the Southern states as the segregation cases slowly mounted toward the Supreme Court. One would prefer to draw only upon this last source but those appeals to biology and theology which the racist employs cannot be left out of the complete picture and they are naturally not to be found in responsible legal briefs. They must be sought elsewhere.

The four cases affected by the decision of May 17, 1954, had come to the Court from two authentically Southern states, Virginia and South Carolina, one border state, Delaware, and one not properly Southern at all, Kansas. It is the first two of these that are most instructive. Kansas concentrated its defense on a strictly legal question, namely, the constitutionality of the state laws of 1879 and 1905 which permitted segregation at local option. In Topeka itself the issue was becoming largely theoretical even before 1954 since in the autumn of 1953 the local Board of Education there had decided to

[31] See William W. Brickman, "Silence and Segregation," *School and Society*, 85 (Nov. 23, 1957), 360. Myron Lieberman in "Civil Rights and the N.E.A.," *School and Society*, 85 (May 11, 1957), 166–169, celebrates the centennial year of the N.E.A. with a compelling indictment of that organization's generally "weak record" in the area of civil rights with particular attention to its vacillations on the segregation issue.

discontinue segregation in its twenty white and four Negro elementary schools "as rapidly as is practicable."

The arguments that have been proposed in defense of the biracial educational system fall into one of three categories according as they deal with matters of law, with matters of fact or with matters of ideology. The legal arguments also have a historical dimension since the effort to prove that the segregation statutes were not unconstitutional pivots on interpretation of the Fourteenth Amendment and the intentions of the 39th Congress regarding it. These arguments loom large in many of the legal briefs but do not particularly affect a philosophy already committed to segregation quite apart from questions of legality. The matters of fact concern the sociological and cultural realities of life in the South. It is ironic to find such Southern spokesmen as James F. Byrnes complaining that the Court based its decision not on law but on sociological evidence, for the states of South Carolina and Virginia themselves adverted to their sociological structure and cultural patterns as arguments against integration and they supported these analyses with appeals to professional authority. In its essence, the sociological argument maintains that the biracial pattern expresses the wishes of both races and is a necessary pillar of public tranquility. It is an argument which appeals most, perhaps, to those who cherish the wistful myth of an Old South that never was, where the time is always late afternoon and the frost beads the silver julep goblets set out on wide verandas.

The ideological rationale is less romantic. It is of a more abstract and general nature and is found only implicitly, if at all, in the briefs for the various appellees. On the other hand, it preoccupies the popular imagination which vibrates so easily, for instance, to talk of miscegenation. This theoretical defense constitutes a kind of philosophy of public education which may be gathered together under the three conventional rubrics of educational aims, agencies, and theory of human nature.

Not infrequently education is defined in some abstract and excessively individualistic way as the process of actualizing all a man's truly human potentialities according to their hierarchic ordering. Actually, no education ever quite does this since different cultures demand the development of different sorts of skills and permit the neglect of others. A child of the Pacific Islands may need the ability to swim great distances under water but not the intellectual sophistication required of a modern urban American. On a realistic view, therefore, what is happening in any education is the transmission by the elders of their way of life to the younger members of their society. This may or may not require a "conservative" school. If that particular way of life places a premium upon traditional etiquette and the *status quo*, that is what will be transmitted. If the adult generation esteems adventuresome or pragmatic qualities, if it encourages inventiveness and a restless zeal for improvement, this, too, will be communicated. From one angle, therefore, it is true that the schools in a given community are the means, to use Dewey's phrase, of the social continuity of life.[32]

This fact is basic to a Southern argument for segregation which runs as follows: Since any education is designed to transmit a way of life it must conform itself to and respect that way of life. But the Southern way of life rests on biracialism and the Southern school must therefore do the same. The minor is buttressed by appeals to the supposed antiquity of the tradition and to the actualities of the contemporary scene. Thus a Brief for the Appellees from Virginia warned the Supreme Court that a ban on segregation would be "to take a long stride into a field where history is clear, traditions are long and emotions are strong."[33] An earlier brief from the same state included quotations from the testimony in a lower court of Dr. Howard, Virginia's Superintendent of Public Instruction who said: "It has been my experience, in working with the people of Virginia including both white and Negro, that the customs and the habits and the traditions

[32] John Dewey, *Democracy and Education* (New York: Macmillan, 1916), p. 3. But this is not a distinctively instrumentalistic view. Thus Christopher Dawson, the distinguished Catholic historian and social thinker, writes: "Taken in its widest sense education is simply the process by which the new members of a community are initiated into its ways of life and thought from the simplest elements of behavior or manners up to the highest tradition of spiritual wisdom."—*Understanding Europe* (New York: Sheed & Ward, 1952), p. 292. None of this is to deny, of course, that the person is himself developed in the educational process. Nor does it mean that individuals exist only for society's sake and require to be totally subordinated to the power of the community.

[33] In the Supreme Court of the United States, October Term, 1953, Brief of Appellees in No. 4 (*Davis* v. *County School Board*) in Reply to Supplemental Brief for the United States on Reargument (Dec. 7, 1953), p. 21.

of Virginia are such that they believe for the best interest of both the white and the Negro that the separate school is best. . . ."[34]

Virginia itself argued that biracialism in education represented "the fixed policies of the several States which are based on local social conditions well known to the respective legislatures." The proof was said to lie in the evidence that Virginians so prize the biracial system that they are prepared to validate their sincerity by bearing its financial pressures.[35] (The questionable character of this proof is suggested by Harlan's study referred to above.) It was urged, moreover, that segregation was itself an engine not only of social stability but also of progressive improvements in the social order. It was described by Virginia's spokesmen as part of the public policy adopted to prevent violence and reduce resentment while South Carolina maintained that the institution of segregation was ensuring the sort of unity which promotes progress whereas integration would destroy that unity.[36]

It may be observed, in reference to this argumentation, that although schools transmit a people's culture they are hardly obliged to perpetuate those of its elements which examination shows to be morally invalid. After all, men and their societies are situated in a historical process and must criticize the direction and the goals of this movement if it is not to become aimless or degenerate. It is im-

[34] In the Supreme Court of the United States, October Term, 1953, Brief of Appellees in No. 4 (*Davis* v. *County School Board*) on Reargument, (Nov. 30, 1953), pp. 69–70. There is reason to suspect that when the Southern white claimed Negroes also favored segregation he was quite misinformed. Commenting on Florida's survey of public opinion, the attorney general of that state in an *Amicus Curiae* brief observed: "It is evident that a vast area of misunderstanding as to each other's feelings about segregation exists between the races. White leaders believe Negroes to be much more satisfied with segregation than Negroes are and Negro leaders believe that whites are much more willing to accept desegregation gracefully than whites proved to be."—*Amicus Curiae Brief of the Attorney General of Florida, op. cit.,* p. 27.

[35] In the Supreme Court of the United States, October Term, 1952, Brief for Appellees in No. 191 (*Davis* v. *County School Board*) (Oct. 9, 1952), pp. 1, 9, 21.

[36] *Ibid.,* p. 17, and see: In the Supreme Court of the United States, October Term, 1952, Brief for Appellees in No. 101 (*Briggs* v. *Elliott*) (Oct. 3, 1952), p. 32. The comment about segregation as a preservative of unity is quoted in this latter brief from words of Colgate W. Darden, Jr., President of the University of Virginia.

possible, besides, to maintain a perfectly static position. The duty of some reconstruction is unavoidable and a community's way of life cannot expect to be perfectly exempt.

Still, it may be asked to whom the work of criticism and reconstruction should be committed. This brings up another key thesis in the Southern philosophy of education, namely, the insistence on the inviolability of the principle of local control. This is, to be sure, part of the American educational creed. The celebrated Article X of the Bill of Rights observed that "the powers not delegated to the United States by the Constitution, nor prohibited by it to the States, are reserved to the States respectively, or to the people." Control of education is perhaps the most significant of these powers. Moreover, American law, like its English progenitor, has traditionally honored the parents' primacy in educational responsibility and the device of local control of the public schools (through the several states' delegation of their power to those local communities) is a sound method of safeguarding this right and rendering its exercise meaningful.

Naturally enough a decided accent on the importance of maintaining local self-government in local affairs is a cornerstone of the Southern theory of educational agencies. A brief from South Carolina under date of October 3, 1952, called this principle:

... essential to the peace and happiness of each locality and to the strength and stability of our whole federal system. Nowhere is this more profoundly true than in the field of education. It is the duty and function of each state primarily to provide for the education of its citizens. To devolve this sensitive activity so far as may be on those to whose minds and hearts it is an intimate concern is surely the highest statesmanship.[37]

An *Amicus Curiae* brief of the attorney general of Maryland was submitted to the Supreme Court in the October Term, 1953. It contains in an Appendix a grass-roots document expressing similar ideas. This is a declaration called "The West River Proclamation," subscribed to by a number of P.T.A.'s in Anne Arundel County. "We believe," it declares in part,

[37] In the Supreme Court of the United States, October Term, 1952, Brief for Appellees in No. 101 (*Briggs* v. *Elliott*) (Oct. 3, 1952), p. 7.

... that among our rights is a direct voice in the education of our children. ... That in order to assure equal protection of the law to each race and to prevent development of an inferiority complex in any child, no child should be compelled to undertake public education under instructors not of his own race without consent of his parents or guardians. ... That the administration of free schools should be conducted on the principle of maximum local control with the objective of the greatest satisfaction to all participating students, subordinating neither the majority to the minority nor the minority to the majority.[38]

This insistence on local control has a certain affinity with the spirit behind the "States' rights" doctrine. It is, consequently, much exploited by a Senator Talmadge. But all such statements labor under a certain failure to distinguish between the right of local control and the right to exercise that control so absolutely as to be subject to no higher scrutiny or review. Yet the validity of such a distinction is apparent from several different angles. The Christian moral theologian would point out, for example, that there can be no real right to wound justice or charity. And the Supreme Court, working within the perspective of constitutional law, has decided that the Fourteenth Amendment did extend over the states many of the restraints imposed upon the federal government by the Bill of Rights. An editorial comment in *America* on the New Orleans trouble put the matter neatly when it observed that there are many advantages in the balance of powers inherent in the dual sovereignty of nation and states but that local autonomy scarcely flourishes when it is made the vehicle for local prejudice and for violations of rights guaranteed by the federal Constitution.[39]

A final group of arguments involves interpretations of human nature itself, interpretations which purport to be rooted in psychology, biology, and theology and to dictate biracial education as necessary and proper. The "psychological argument" is for the most part in-

[38] In the Supreme Court of the United States, October Term, 1953, *Amicus Curiae* of the Attorney General of Maryland in Nos. 1, 2, 4 and 10 (*Brown* v. *Board of Education of Topeka, Briggs* v. *Elliott, Davis* v. *County Board of Prince Edward County, Virginia, Gebhart* v. *Belton*), Edward D. E. Rollins, Attorney General of Maryland. P. App. 62.

[39] Editorial, "Betrayal of States' Rights," *America,* 104 (December 17, 1960), 392–393.

offensive except when stained with racism. It is expressed in generalized references, for example, to a worthy "pride of race." In a talk at Bennetsville, South Carolina, September 26, 1957, former Governor Byrnes remarked that Negroes had just been acquiring this pride when the Court intervened with its talk of inferiority complexes. Then there are those vague appeals to a supposed "universal consciousness of kind" and the degrees of visibility of difference between races.[40] More persuasive, if no better substantiated empirically, was Virginia's claim that "amalgamation" could be successful only at the graduate school level where one might expect to find a maturity and an independence of parental prejudices not likely in high school students.[41] Actually, a number of careful observers have concluded that integration may work best with young children. But in any event there is a phantom lurking here that will not be easily exorcized. It is conjured up by the fear of miscegenation linked to the presumption that adolescents are particularly vulnerable to its supposed allure.

Perhaps the theme of racism with its two strands—the doctrine of the Negro's genetic inferiority and the conviction that he intends to overcome it by intermarriage—is really nuclear in the South's philosophy of education. It does not, of course, intrude directly into the legal briefs of the Southern states although its presence may be detected even there. But in the *Amicus Curiae* from Maryland, mentioned above, the racialistic note is clearly sounded in a copy of the "Petition Circulated by the Maryland Petition Committee" which the Brief prints in its grab bag of appendices:

We believe that the heritage of our race is the one gift received from our ancestors which we may with surety transmit to our children. We believe that this God given heritage should not be taken from us by any human law or decision. We believe that it is the duty of judicial, legislative and execu-

[40] See: In the Supreme Court of the United States, October Term, 1952, Brief for Appellees in No. 101 (*Briggs* v. *Elliott*) (October 3, 1952), p. 31, which cites a speech by Dr. Frank P. Graham, former president of the University of North Carolina, who spoke of ". . . the origin, history, and power of the 'mores' of peoples based on the universal consciousness of kind, of historic social heritage, the degree of visibility of the difference between races. . . ."

[41] In the Supreme Court of the United States, October Term, 1952, Brief for Appellees in No. 191 (*Davis* v. *County School Board*), *op. cit.*, p. 10.

tive agencies to protect this heritage, not to move for its destruction. We believe that the abolition of segregation in our school strikes through our children, at the survival of our race, because it deprives them of protection which they need until they develop adult judgment.[42]

Newspaper reports and on-the-spot surveys like Martin's *The Deep South Says "Never"* have shown how widespread this sort of thinking is. Naturally enough, young people themselves reflect it. The transcript of a panel discussion involving seven students, four white and three Negro, from Little Rock's Central High School, in October, 1957, showed how the topic inevitably arises. A white girl remarked in the course of the conversation that she thought her friends' objection to the Negro pupils was based on opposition to "race-mixing" which she defined as "marrying each other." Some of the other panelists, both white and Negro, pointed out that this was not the motive of the Negro students. "Why do I want to go to school," said a Negro boy, "to marry with someone? I mean, school's not a marriage bureau. . . . I'm going there for an education."[43]

Ostensibly the objection to intermarriage is based upon the conviction, previously indicated, that the Negro is naturally inferior and hence genetically adapted for an inferior role whereas miscegenation would mean, in Judge Brady's genial phrase, "mongrelization," blowing out the light in the white man's brain and muddying his skin. The scientific pretensions of such racism have been thoroughly exploded by studies in anthropology and differential psychology. Unfortunately, this pseudo-scientific doctrine remains a dynamic if somewhat intangible factor in the segregation debate. In the South, it is sometimes haloed by a gratuitous linkage to a pseudo theology. This is a rhetorical sort of device with something of a history. In 1866, for instance, when the Arkansas Legislature was debating the possibility of "mixed schools," a certain Mr. Bradley demanded to know whether his colleagues meant to force the poor who could not afford private education to thrust their children "for three months in the year, among the offspring of a race whom God, by writing an indelible mark upon their head and foot and brain, has pronounced the social

[42] *Amicus Curiae* brief of the attorney general of Maryland, *op. cit.*, pp. App. 63–64. This brief also includes a number of statements by Maryland citizens who supported the decision abolishing educational segregation.
[43] *The New York Times,* Oct. 20, 1957, p. E 7.

inferiors of your sons and daughters."[44] This horrifying sentiment
would perhaps be expressed more circumspectly today—in legislatures and courts, at least—but it still flourishes and Senator Talmadge
can entitle one section of his little book, "God Advocates Segregation." A similar theme characterized the statement which two Georgia
lawyers prepared as an *Amicus Curiae* brief in the case from South
Carolina although it was not actually admitted as such by the Court.
Biblical references are distributed throughout its rambling pages. The
reader is told that the ancient Jewish people believed in keeping their
tribe pure and so do the people of the Bible Belt today, including
the Negroes. Ethnologists may insist that these devout fundamental-
ists are wrong in believing that Ham, Noah's disrespectful son, was the
"progenitor of the colored race." But this dispute simply reminds the
two lawyers of the hoary witticism about the bumblebee. "By all the
laws of aerodynamics he cannot fly, but he has never studied aerodynamics. So he flies anyhow, and does a good job of it. Maybe the
ethnologists are wrong."[45]

The Christian conscience, it is hardly necessary to say, can only
be deeply distressed to see distorted religious convictions bent to the
service of racism. Actually, as another chapter in this book shows,
the authentic theological judgment on the interracial question quite
destroys the theses of the segregationist. Indeed, it can be easily
demonstrated that the imperatives of Christianity in this whole matter far outreach even that celebrated decision of May 17, 1954.

[44] Quoted in: In the Supreme Court of the United States, October Term, Supplemental Brief for the United States in Nos. 1, 2, 4, 8, and 10 in Reargument, p.
172.

[45] Louis L. Brown and Robert W. Wesley, In the Supreme Court of the
United States, brief *Amicus Curiae* in *Briggs* v. *Elliott*, n.d., p. 29.

The Law and the Negro in the North

ROBERT F. DRINAN

When a group of Jamestown, Virginia, tobacco farmers in the year 1620 "purchased" the first cargo of slaves kidnaped from West Africa they could hardly have anticipated that from this original immoral act there would emerge America's greatest moral dilemma. Nor could these Southern merchants have anticipated that Anglo-American law, one of the greatest creations of civilized man, would fail to render basic justice to this new group of human beings who in 1860 would number 3 million and in 1961 almost 20 million or 11 per cent of the total population.

In 1808 the United States Congress made it a federal crime to import slaves but the federal government did nothing about the legal status of the slaves already here—a group which in 1800 accounted for one-fifth of the new nation's total inhabitants. The inhabitants of African descent remained without a legal status and as salable as a bale of cotton until after the War Between the States.

The United States Supreme Court three times in major decisions denied the full protection of the Constitution to Negroes—in the Dred Scott opinion prior to the Civil War, in the decision in 1883 nullifying the Civil Rights Acts and in the ruling in *Plessy* v. *Ferguson*[1] in 1896 sustaining the "separate but equal" doctrine.

Clearly as a direct result of the Supreme Court's refusal from the 1860's until 1954 to grant full equality to all citizens in the South, the Negroes have migrated out of the South into the North in vast numbers. In 1900 only 10 per cent of the Negro population lived outside the South; today at least 40 per cent do. Since 1940 3 million Negroes have left the South.[2]

It is possible that during the sixties more than half of the nation's Negroes will reside in the North. The "colored problem" therefore is by no means confined to the seventeen states which maintained "Jim Crow" legislation prior to 1954 but has been extended to Northern cities. In fact the influx of Negroes into the cities of the North— accompanied simultaneously by a vast movement of whites into the suburbs—is creating a situation unique in American history—the possibility of a large minority Negro voting group controlling the politics of a city whose metropolitan population is overwhelmingly non-Negro.

LAW AND THE NORTHERN STATES

With remarkable wisdom and liberality many Northern cities and states initiated a series of antidiscrimination laws soon after World War II. The value of these laws, which now exist to some extent in one-third of our states, is difficult to evaluate. The relative novelty of these laws, as well as the widely varying patterns of enforcement, necessarily cause even the most ardent foe of discrimination to be cautious in his enthusiasm concerning the effectiveness of such laws.

No one can dispute, however, that these new laws against discrimination in education, employment, housing, and other areas have an undeniably beneficial effect in educating all citizens concerning a

[1] 163 U.S. 537 (1896).
[2] *Newsweek*, Dec. 23, 1957.

clearly stated public policy. The educative function of civil war—a
neglected area of research in jurisprudence—is operative in the antidiscrimination laws in a way seldom if ever witnessed in American
law.

It is furthermore beyond dispute that the promoters and authors
of the vast proliferation of statutes and regulations forbidding discrimination, which the North has enacted during the last decade, seek
to elevate the moral standards of the community by law. Not every
jurist will concede that law can or should expect to be able to achieve
such a lofty objective. And today, in fact, one would surmise that the
philosophy of legal realism which has so dominated this generation
of American lawyers and judges would not be enthusiastic or even
willing to legislate an "ought" over the accepted "is."

A legal attempt to change the face of society by "integrating" two
groups is a completely new experience not merely for American law
but also for the Anglo-American common law—from which American
law derives—and which now constitutes the basic legal foundation of
the vast newly independent nations within the British Common-
wealth. In times past all sorts of immigrant groups in America have
been assimilated without need of a new body of law. The Negro
problem, however, is different and unique. Since widespread interracial intermarriage seems to continue as an impossible eventuality,
the "integration" of the Negro "race" will not be that assimilation
which has characterized the absorption of every other group in American history.

The Negro "race" poses for the first time an unprecedented situation in American pluralism. In the last century the American people
saw a comparable problem arising from the growing number of Ori-
entals on the West Coast and America moved promptly to eliminate
the problem by outlawing late in the last century *all* immigration from
Oriental countries. The Negro "race," however, was here before the
formation of the Union and today presents to the nation its foremost
problem in pluralism.

Other minorities besides Negroes have been included in antidiscrimination laws but the problem of equality for Negroes in the
North is so overwhelmingly more important and urgent than that of
any other minority that it deserves special treatment. Discrimination

based on religion or national origin or age, however unfortunate, is more easily overcome by reason and diminished by conciliation than the deeply imbedded discrimination against Negroes which scars every Northern city.

It has been estimated that the city of Chicago may be as much as 50 per cent Negro within a decade. Comparable predictions could possibly be made for other Northern cities. At what point should law and society begin in order to destroy the ghettoes which, on a "checkerboard" pattern, proclaim in silence the unspoken hostility of a white majority? Housing, education, and employment are the three large areas where *de facto* segregation enters the lives of virtually all of the Negroes in the North. On which area is it more important to concentrate? If housing is desegregated, will education and employment follow? Or is integrated education more important in the long run? Or is the way of living of the vast majority of Negroes preestablished by the types of employment open to them?

The law has not formulated any clear answers to these questions which involve complex issues of economics, sociology, urban renewal, and public opinion. But the law has tried to lend its sanction to the outlawing of bias in many areas; whether the new laws in the North against discrimination are the cause or the effect of the virtually universal proclamations by the press and public officials against discrimination is a question which only posterity can answer. But, it is certain that the antidiscrimination statutes now in effect in sixteen states[3] will deepen and be benefited by the growing consciousness in the North, both by Negroes and by whites, that true equality for Negroes is an ideal and not a reality in almost all Northern cities.

Discrimination in Housing

Without trying to decide where the center of the web of bias resides it will be profitable to consider discrimination in housing, education, and employment beginning with the widespread denial of equal housing opportunities to some 27.5 million Americans because

[3] The sixteen states with antidiscrimination statutes are: Alaska, California, Colorado, Connecticut, Massachusetts, Michigan, Minnesota, New Jersey, New Mexico, New York, Ohio, Oregon, Pennsylvania, Rhode Island, Washington, Wisconsin.

of race or other reasons.[4] Negroes are the most universally disadvantaged. Eight state antidiscrimination agencies have been given jurisdiction to enforce laws against discrimination in housing.[5] But only four of these states have any legal ban on the sale or leasing of private, non-publicly assisted housing.[6]

It is likely that laws against discrimination in housing will increase rapidly within the next few years. The Catholic hierarchy in its annual statement in 1958 implicitly urged more laws of this nature when it condemned unequal treatment in "all public and semipublic facilities." The nation's realtors, in their official code of ethics promulgated by the National Association of Real Estate Boards, have recently dropped a provision authorizing the exclusion of minorities "whose presence will clearly be detrimental to property values in the neighborhood."

Law, however, is but one of many powerful forces operating on the complex situation which results from the desire of Negroes to move out of the city "ghetto" and the determination of the whites not to allow their community to change its basic racial pattern. Real estate officials have named the process by which whites leave areas of Negro in-migration as "tipping the neighborhood." Once the proportion of Negroes exceeds the limits of the neighborhood's tolerance for interracial living the whites move out.[7]

Quakers in the Philadelphia suburbs, conscientiously seeking to create and make permanent a truly interracial community, have tried to control rigidly the proportion of Negroes so that the neighborhood will not "tip"—causing an out-migration of whites. The only interracial communities in the United States are those where, through economic or social pressure, there exists a limit upon the influx of non-whites. In view of this fact, state laws banning all discrimination and promoting "open-occupancy" housing go beyond the public opinion

[4] See "Discrimination in Housing" by Eunice and George Grier, published by Anti-Defamation League, 1960. See also "Residence and Race," report of the Commission on Race and Housing (University of California Press, 1958).

[5] The eight states are: Colorado, Connecticut, Massachusetts, New Jersey, New York, Oregon, Rhode Island, Washington.

[6] The four states are: Colorado, Connecticut, Massachusetts, Oregon.

[7] For a most penetrating study of the complex forces at work in urban-suburban housing see "The Metropolitan Area as a Racial Problem" by Morton Grodzins (University of Pittsburgh Press, 1958).

of the white majority which will not at this time submit to living in a community which has passed beyond a certain point in its Negro population.

Could a law be drafted that would realistically provide for the creation and maintenance of a community on an interracial basis? Could zoning laws be devised that would bring whites back into the city and allow Negroes to choose freely where they want to live in the suburbs? The law is a novice in this area and, because it must be uniform and constitutional, has up to this time simply reiterated a demand for equality of treatment.

Obviously some widespread desire for an interracial community as a desirable thing must precede its realization. At the present time even the most ardent advocates of civic equality must concede that a serious problem is confronted by the property owner who feels that he may suffer a severe financial loss if he fails to sell his realty before a neighborhood changes its racial pattern. Although there is solid evidence that the influx of Negroes or other minority groups does not depreciate the property values of the neighborhood,[8] the fact is that such alleged depreciation is a commonly accepted belief among property owners. In order to meet this problem in a Christian way the following striking statement was adopted by the 168th General Assembly of the Presbyterian Church of America in 1956:

The . . . Assembly calls upon Christians who are contemplating the sale of property to see as of first importance the need of minority families for equal housing opportunities and . . . to make their houses available to all qualified purchasers without regard to race.[9]

Few if any church groups have been this specific about the morality of working against Negroes in their attempts to upgrade the quality of their housing and neighborhood. It is to be hoped that Catholic moral theologians will seek to clarify the duties of sellers of property and the rights of minority buyers of property.

An excellent handbook on this general subject is "A Guide to Chang-

---

[8] See "Guide to Changing Neighborhoods" (pp. 28–30) published by the National Community Relations Advisory Council, 1956.

[9] Cited at p. 55 in "Where Shall We Live?", Report of the Commission on Race and Housing (University of California Press, 1958).

ing Neighborhoods."[10] Both the contents and the bibliography of this study reveal the profound historic, economic, and sociological problems involved in racial attitudes toward integrated neighborhoods. The complexity of the situation is compounded by the fact that Negro families dwell in the very areas of the nation's blighted cities most in need of the urban renewal assistance available under the 1954 Housing Act.[11] If better housing is constructed to replace slum conditions, will the new and more attractive neighborhood keep nonwhites within the same area to such an extent that whites will not reenter the cities?[12]

Although Catholic groups—especially the National Conference of Catholic Interracial Councils—have been very active in combating discrimination in every form it seems fair to say that Catholic teaching and practice on interracial housing has been less satisfactory than Catholic teaching and practice on any other aspect of the racial problem.

The next few years will afford many opportunities for Catholics to display in the area of housing the sentiment expressed by Pius XII when, writing to the American bishops, he said: "We confess that we feel special paternal affection, which is certainly inspired of heaven for the Negro people dwelling among you. . . ."[13] All Catholics, and especially priests, were again forcefully reminded of their opportunities by Albert Cardinal Meyer, Archbishop of Chicago, in his call for "moral leadership for eliminating racial discrimination from the whole community." Cardinal Meyer warned against regarding the Negro "solely as an object of conversion" and affirmed that "we must

[10] Published in 1956 by the National Community Relations Advisory Council, 9 East 38th St., New York 16, N.Y.

[11] See Hearing Before the United States Commission on Civil Rights, Housing, Vol. 2, June 10, 1959, Washington, D.C., pp. 2–8.

[12] For a thorough analysis of the law and discrimination see: "The Right to Equal Treatment: Administrative Enforcement of Antidiscrimination Legislation," 74 *Harvard Law Review,* 529–590 (1960). The cautious conclusion of the co-authors is as follows: ". . . many feel that the ultimate solution to the problems of racial and religious discrimination lies with education and not with legal compulsion. Experience indicates, however, that without the force of law to nourish it along, the right to equal treatment will develop slowly, if at all" (p. 589).

For a complete review of statutes and decisions see "The Law and Discrimination in Housing" by Loren Miller, 20 *Lawyers Guild Review,* 123–136 (1960).

[13] *Sertum Laetitiae,* Nov. 1, 1939.

never lose sight of his needs as a human being, his legitimate desire to be accepted with dignity into the fabric of society generally."[14]

A progressive statement seeking to implement these ideals was made in early 1961 by the Pennsylvania Catholic Welfare Conference, a group representing the Catholic bishops of that state. This statement urged enactment in Pennsylvania of Senate Bill No. 53 which would outlaw discrimination in *private* housing. An endorsement of legislation of this nature by an Episcopal body of the Church seems to be a new if not a unique event in Catholic life in America.

EDUCATION AND NEGROES IN THE NORTH

Residential desegregation in Northern cities would probably bring about integration in the schools. In the present state of things, however, what is and what should be the educational pattern for the children of Northern Negroes?

There seems to be consensus that probably twice as many colored children do not finish high school as white children.[15] In the seventeen Southern and border states, which in June, 1960, enrolled in integrated schools 181,020 Negro children or 6 per cent of the 3,020,727 Negro school population of the area, the number of nonwhite pupils who fail to finish high school is undoubtedly much higher.[16]

Negroes in the North have been increasingly more discontented with schools where the population is overwhelmingly nonwhite. Three law suits petitioning school boards for arrangements to produce more integration in the public schools have, however, failed. In Pennsylvania and in Michigan Federal Courts judges have ruled that the construction of a school in an area of heavy Negro population did not necessarily imply discrimination.[17] In a New York case the judge, although recognizing that there was *de facto* segregation in the public schools in question, found that this was due to the geography involved

[14] *The New York Times,* Jan. 29, 1961.

[15] "Half a Life," pamphlet (n.d.) issued by National Urban League, Inc.

[16] See 30 *Harvard Educational Review,* 209, Summer, 1960, Special Issue on "Negro Education in the United States."

[17] *Sealy* v. *Department of Public Instruction,* 159 F. Supp., (Penna. ——— 1959 ———), affirmed 252 F. 2nd 898.

and not to discrimination. The judge ruled that parents could not justifiably withdraw their children from such schools on the basis that they were being denied equal educational rights.[18]

A new and possibly revolutionary phase of the law on equal educational opportunities was opened when on January 24, 1961 Judge Irving R. Kaufman issued a unique opinion ruling that the town of New Rochelle had failed to carry out the Supreme Court's 1954 desegregation mandate. The charge: New Rochelle still operates a primary school where 94 per cent of the students are colored. The presence in this school of 29 white children does not, Judge Kaufman ruled, afford the 454 Negro children enrolled the "educational and social contacts and interaction envisioned" by the *Brown* decision of the Supreme Court.[19]

Although an appeal from this decision has been taken by New Rochelle officials the case and the opinion pose in a striking way the dilemma of Northern educational officials—is there placed upon these authorities an obligation to neutralize and even reverse in public schools the many and powerful forces which draw or drive Negroes into residential areas which are or become overwhelmingly Negro? Must or should educational officials adjust school schedules and districts so as to maximize racial integration and thereby give to white and Negro children the cultural advantage of mingling freely? To what extent is the Negro pupil being deprived of his right to a good education simply by being enrolled in a *de facto* segregated school?

The Board of Education of the City of New York in 1954, pursuant to the finding by the Public Education Association of "serious and persistent inferiority" in *de facto* segregated schools, adopted a declaration of policy in line with the PEA conclusions. The policy aimed at elevating standards in schools in heavily Negro areas up to citywide levels and, by appropriate site and zoning selection, to decrease the amount of actual segregation. Although the implementation of this policy has not always been satisfactory to all observers its adoption is of great significance.[20]

The attorney general of New Jersey, arguing in a 1954 case, urged

18 *In Re Skipworth*, 180 NYS 2nd 852 1958.
19 See excerpts of opinion in *The New York Times*, Jan. 25, 1961, p. 24.
20 "Schools, Courts, and the Negro's Future," by John A. Morsell, 30 *Harvard Educational Review* 181 (1960).

that the state's Law Against Discrimination should be construed to prohibit a "board of education from permitting the existence of segregation-in-fact when it can reasonably be limited."[21]

If the directive of the New Jersey attorney general is to become the law then many school officials in Northern cities have a great deal of segregation-in-fact to eliminate. According to a survey made by the American Jewish Congress[22] 87 per cent of Chicago's Negro elementary school children attend schools that are "to all intent and purposes Negro schools." The same survey reveals that 43 of Los Angeles' elementary schools have Negro enrollments of 85 per cent or more and that in Philadelphia 14 per cent of the public elementary schools have Negro enrollments of more than 99 per cent!

Although New York, Baltimore, and Philadelphia have experimented with an "open-enrollment" policy which permits students to transfer out of their neighborhoods most other cities apparently have taken no action designed to alter the pattern of educational segregation which characterizes many Northern cities. Public school officials in Princeton, New Jersey, have, however, not adopted the usual defense of administrators who justify the perpetuation of segregation by saying that the school board, like the law, is "color-blind." Princeton authorities admit that they are "color-conscious" and as a result two nearby schools—one in a predominantly Negro area and another attended primarily by white children—have been reclassified so that one school is attended by children in the lower grades while the other is attended by children in the upper grades. The result is genuine interracial integration.

The New Rochelle case presents an excellent illustration of the difficulties which suburban school boards confront when they try to implement the directives of the Public Education Association and the New Jersey attorney general. The school board of New Rochelle asserts that an entire section of that town is inhabited almost exclusively by Negroes. Even if a directive is issued authorizing Negro children currently in the 97 per cent Negro Lincoln school to go to nearby

---

[21] *Ibid.*, p. 183–184.
See also "Race Relations and American Law," Jack Greenberg (Columbia University Press, 1959). On the effects of *de facto* segregated education on Negro children see "The Negro Potential," Eli Ginzberg (Columbia University Press, 1956).
[22] See synopsis in *The New York Times*, Feb. 22, 1961.

schools they will, according to the Board, still be enrolled in schools which have a high concentration of Negro children. Must New Rochelle and other such communities make an effort to disregard the residential segregation of its Negro population and have fully biracial schools? Can this be done without bringing Negro children into a somewhat artificial environment during their school hours after which they return to a neighborhood which is not interracial in any way?

Judge Kaufman's strong opinion in the New Rochelle case asserted, correctly or otherwise, that the Board of Education of that city had "gerrymandered" school districts in order to perpetuate "district lines which were established in the first place out of a desire to separate whites and Negroes." Judge Kaufman, furthermore, finds that in the *Brown* decision there was "necessarily implied ... the positive obligation of eliminating segregation."

How shall school officials be judged as to their fulfillment of this "positive obligation?" In Judge Kaufman's view the "motivation" involved is the crucial question. He states that "if a board of education enters into a course of conduct motivated by a purposeful desire to perpetuate and maintain a segregated school, the constitutional rights of those confined within this segregated establishment have been violated."

The judge goes on, however, to add that his decision does *not* mean that the New Rochelle officials are "segregationists or racists ... but that they have failed to accept or recognize their moral and legal responsibilities." He attributes this failure to an alleged yielding to "pressures of certain groups who wish to avoid an influx of Negro children into the schools of their districts."

One cannot but sympathize with Judge Kaufman's broad interpretation and support of the *Brown* opinion. But if school boards are required to desegregate schools—even by extraordinary means—does it not follow logically that zoning boards and other public officials be required to take comparable means to desegregate housing? It is true that the Supreme Court has never ruled that equality of housing has the same constitutional sanctity as equality of education but logically the first cannot really be expected without the second. And perhaps—even more fundamentally—should not the state really insist on equality in employment opportunities before it can require equality in education? Human equality is socially indivisible.

The future of the Negro in the North—in housing, education, and employment—will be determined to a large degree by what the courts and the white majority believe concerning the deleterious effects of segregation, even though it be *de facto* rather than *de jure*. It is significant in this connection to note that the American hierarchy, in its statement on November 13, 1958, on the Negro question, asserted that "legal segregation, *or any form of compulsory segregation, in itself and by its very nature imposes a stigma of inferiority upon the segregated people*"[23] (emphasis supplied).

Segregated schools arising from geography rather than discrimination would seem to be a "form of compulsory segregation" in the sense that discrimination and segregation in housing and employment are the real causes of segregated schools. It seems to follow therefore that the weight of the hierarchy's authority is added to the famous words of Chief Justice Earl Warren in the *Brown* decision in which he expressed the conviction that segregation of Negro children, especially in their formative years, "generates a feeling of inferiority as to their status in the community that may affect their hearts and minds in a way unlikely ever to be undone."

If sociologists and psychologists continue to produce more evidence of the disastrous consequences upon the human personality of "compulsory segregation" they may well supply the most useful argument that law and society can present in their struggle to eliminate "separate but equal" schools. If prejudice and class hostility are fostered by racial segregation in any form and for whatever reason, then is it not the duty of the law to seek its elimination?[24]

It is not possible to predict how soon Northern school authorities will be forced or will voluntarily adopt a policy of "open admission" in their schools. It is to be hoped in any event that litigation will be avoided if at all possible because, as Judge Kaufman wrote in his New Rochelle opinion:

[23] 57 *Catholic Mind* 85 (1959).
[24] See R. K. Merton, "Discrimination and the American Creed" in R. M. MacIver, ed., *Discrimination and National Welfare*.

Litigation is an unsatisfactory way to resolve issues such as have been presented here. It is costly, time-consuming—causing further delays in the implementation of constitutional rights—and further inflames the emotions of the partisans.

Regardless of the merits of the conflicting claims of the litigants in New Rochelle, one cannot be unmindful of the impact which such litigation must have on the minds and hearts of every Negro adult and child who is involved or who reads of it. Negroes know that there exists a great question about their social acceptability in the golf and beach clubs, in the social and even civic activities of suburbia. Negroes inevitably ponder on the basis of the fear and anxiety that causes even the very best people in suburban society to ignore or even decry the presence of their new nonwhite neighbors. One can imagine the suspicions and apprehensions of Negroes in the suburbs concerning the proceedings of civic bodies and private groups at which the "Negro problem" is discussed.

The outcome of the New Rochelle case and similar litigation across the nation may be more important than can be appreciated at this time. After the U.S. Supreme Court in 1896 in *Plessy* v. *Ferguson* declared that "separate but equal" facilities for Negroes were constitutional, the South settled down to an unprecedented era of "white supremacy." Before 1896 "Jim Crow" legislation had not been nearly so firmly entrenched as it became after the nation's highest court ruled it permissible. There is abundant evidence to indicate that, if the Supreme Court had agreed in 1896 with Justice Harlan's prophetic dissent, the equality of the Negro would have come about much more rapidly after 1896 than it has following sixty more years of "white supremacy."

If higher courts and even the U.S. Supreme Court read into *Brown* what Judge Kaufman did, a whole new horizon is open to Northern Negroes. If the supreme law of the land imposes "a positive obligation of eliminating segregation" on school boards, then one can anticipate eventually the elimination of segregated-in-fact schools. If, on the other hand, the law asserts that a school board may insist that students attend a school within the neighborhood where they reside, a new and powerful impulse may be given to segregated schools in the North.

No statement by a Catholic group on *de facto* segregated schools has been discovered by this writer. Apparently the problem has not been one of concern for Catholic spokesmen.

Because of the very small number of Negro Catholics there will probably be no problem of racial integration in Northern Catholic schools. In fact, there may exist the possibility that the public schools of the North will gradually have a normal number of Negro children and that Catholic schools, because of the paucity of Negro Catholic children, may have virtually no Negro students. If it is deemed to be an advantage for white children to have the companionship in school of nonwhite children, should Catholic schools encourage and even recruit such children?

The status of the Negro in the North can hardly rise above the educational level attainable by the average member of the Negro race. Since Catholics form such a substantial part of the population of Northern cities and have as a result such a powerful voice in the conduct of urban affairs, it is to be hoped that an ever more enlightened Catholic laity will propose and implement all possible reasonable plans to equalize educational opportunities for the Negro in the North.

At the present time it is widely believed that the Catholic Church has furnished outstanding leadership in promoting desegregation in the South. It cannot truly be said that Catholic leadership is thought to be present in the North to the same extent. The area of Northern public elementary and secondary schools—where Catholics are engaged in a teaching and administrative capacity to a greater extent than in most other professions—offers a unique challenge and opportunity. The response to that challenge during the sixties may well constitute in 1970 the most important element in the average Negro's attitude towards the Catholic Church.

EQUALITY IN EMPLOYMENT FOR NORTHERN NEGROES

There are two opposing viewpoints on the present economic status of the Negro. There is much evidence to support the theory that the economic advancement of the Negro race from its plight in 1865 to its present position constitutes one of the most rapid and sensational advancements of any people at any time. The record of ability and

achievement written by the Negro people in the face of enormous opposition is one that could not be easily duplicated.

It is well to see the full force of this argument as one contemplates
the other point of view which stresses the shameful discrimination and
hostility which has always confronted and still confounds the American Negro in his heroic struggle to attain that economic equality
which should be the privilege of every citizen.

Intimately involved in the present and future employment pattern
of the Northern Negro is the general health of the American economy.
The labor shortages caused by the war and the generally vigorous
state of the economy during the fifties have been major factors in
opening up to the Negro new employment opportunities. On the
other hand, recessions with rising unemployment still continue to have
a more disastrous effect on the nonwhite workers than on white employees.

It is well to understand the profound economic forces operating
against unskilled or semiskilled employees before one attempts to
evaluate laws prohibiting bias in hiring. In January, 1961, for example,
13.8 per cent of all Negroes in the labor force were out of work compared with 7 per cent of white workers.[25] This means that in January,
1961, 1,200,000 Negroes were unemployed out of a total in the nation
of 5,385,000 jobless persons. These facts by themselves, however, do
not necessarily prove bias in hiring. One could possibly demonstrate
that they merely mean that all less skilled workers suffer first in an
economic recession.

That discrimination exists in employment, however, is beyond dispute. Patterns of discrimination, moreover, tend to form a vicious
circle; Negroes do not acquire the skills to enter a field where there
is known to be discrimination—thus deepening the wall of separation
between whites and nonwhites in this area. On the other hand, a
disproportionate number of Negroes tend to enter an occupation
where there has been a significant "break-through."

During the last generation the law—at best a clumsy instrument
with which to channel and control the dynamic driving forces of a
restless society—has struggled to promote the ideal of equality in
employment. It was a pragmatic consideration rather than any al-

[25] Report in *The New York Times,* February 18, 1961, of an address by Sec-
retary of Labor Arthur J. Goldberg.

truistic motivation that brought about the first Federal action to equalize employment opportunities for Negroes. In 1941, during a period of increasing labor shortages because of the war, there remained an unutilized source of unemployed Negroes; these individuals had been kept out of expanding defense industries because of deeply imbedded customs of racial exclusion. The depression had added to the forces preventing many Negroes from rising above their customary menial jobs as porters, waiters, and unskilled workers.

The ironic situation of the coexistence of large Negro unemployment with acute labor shortages was taken up by President Roosevelt's cabinet and a directive was issued to Mayor La Guardia of New York, head of Civilian Defense, to consult with Negro officials and prepare an executive order forbidding racial discrimination in employment by any company holding defense orders. With the cooperation of A. Philip Randolph, president of the Brotherhood of Sleeping Car Porters, the only Negro vice president of the American Federation of Labor and the nation's "prime mover" for equal employment opportunities for all citizens, Mr. La Guardia prepared the historic Executive Order 8802 which was issued by the President on June 25, 1941.[26] This directive, establishing the first Fair Employment Practices Committee, is probably one of the finest examples available of what moral leadership from the White House can achieve. The FEPC, because of its imagination and idealism, was to be the spark that ignited a whole movement—a movement that would result in similar committees now in operation in almost twenty states.

In 1941–1942 the first FEPC held public hearings during which it became clear that seven out of ten Negroes in the North believed that they were being discriminated against in war work. In the South, on the other hand, only 7 per cent of the whites were willing to give Negroes equal opportunities for employment and only 12 per cent approved equal wages for Negroes for equal work.[27]

In 1943, as manpower shortages mounted, the Administration had to decide how extensively and vigorously it should carry on its struggle to compel compliance with its executive order designed to outlaw

[26] 6 Fed. Reg. 3109 (1941).
[27] See *Discrimination—U.S.A.*, Jacob K. Javits, 1960, (Harcourt, Brace & Co.), pp. 78–99.

discrimination in government contracts. On May 27, 1943, the White House issued Executive Order 9346 requiring a clause in all government contracts forbidding employment discrimination and appointing a new committee with a full-time chairman and adequate funds to investigate complaints of noncompliance.

The late Bishop (then Monsignor), Francis J. Haas, professor, author, and conciliation expert, was named chairman of the new committee. With great tact and in confrontation with militant opposition from Southern leaders in Congress, Monsignor Haas, with the assistance of his distinguished committee, conducted hearings and issued reports which helped to upgrade the Negro's industrial status. Perhaps more importantly, Monsignor Haas's committee informed the American people about the deep-seated resistance to employing or promoting Negro workers.

Southern Congressional leaders scored a major victory when, at the end of the war, they promptly succeeded in putting FEPC out of existence. The example and achievements of this committee, however, were noted by the states as, for example, in New York where in 1944 a governor's Committee on Discrimination in Employment proposed legislation to outlaw discrimination even in private employment.[28] The measure failed to pass but its message and echo were destined to be heard in New York and most Northern states. A year later, on March 12, 1945, Governor Dewey signed the first state law against discrimination in private employment in American history. Like the FEPC it was conceived in war and, while motivated by a pragmatic desire to augment the labor force, nonetheless asserted that "the opportunity to obtain employment without discrimination . . . is hereby recognized and declared to be a civil right."[29]

The first American statute proscribing bias on the part of private employers established a State Commission against Discrimination (SCAD) to implement the purposes of the law. The effectiveness and educational power of SCAD was so impressive to other states that by 1959 a total of sixteen states had enacted some form of statute outlawing unfair practices in employment. These sixteen states with

[28] See Report, New York State War Council, Committee on Discrimination in Employment, March 1941, to July, 1944.
[29] See Art. 15, Sect. 290–301, Laws of 1951, Ch. 800.

FEPC laws contain 50 per cent of the nation's citizens and almost 25 per cent of its Negro population.[30]

Another Federal impetus to the movement to enact legal controls over group bias came in 1953 when President Eisenhower established the President's Committee on Government Contracts consisting of fifteen members under the chairmanship of Vice President Nixon.[31] The committee, the outgrowth of President Truman's Committee on Government Contracts,[32] never enjoyed statutory authority and hence received neither appropriations nor the power to subpoena witnesses. Although the federal government spends more than thirty billion dollars annually in some six million contracts the government has never had adequate legal machinery to compel compliance with the nondiscrimination clause written into each of these contracts.[33]

A vigorous enforcement policy on the part of the federal government of its nondiscrimination clause would probably achieve more for equality in employment than any other imaginable event. The ban against bias in hiring for work on government contracts extends to subcontractors and thus touches virtually every industrial plant in the nation.[34]

It is not certain to legal authorities how the government could most effectively exact compliance with the anti-bias clause. Can the government declare a breach of contract or seek injunctive relief or request liquidated damages or deny other contracts to companies who discriminate in their employment policies?[35] It seems clear that federal action would be more effective if the President's 1959 recommendation to give statutory authority to the Committee on Government Contracts had been included in the Civil Rights Bill of 1960. The Administration's proposal in this regard was defeated in the course of the debate in the Senate, amid emotional addresses which

[30] An excellent early study of antidiscrimination laws is had in "Equality by Statute: Legal Controls over Group Discrimination" by Morroe Berger (Columbia University Press, 1952).

[31] Executive Order 10479 as amended by Executive Order 10482 (1953).

[32] Executive Order No. 10308 (1951).

[33] 5 *Race Relations Law Reporter* 575 (Summer, 1960).

[34] See 1 *Race Relations Law Reporter* 458 (1956).

[35] See "The Nondiscrimination Clause in Government Contracts," 43 *Virginia Law Review* 837 (1957). See also "The Government Blacklist: Debarment and Suspension of Bidders on Government Contracts," 25 *George Washington Law Review* 175 (1957).

demonstrate all too vividly that anything resembling a federal FEPC will still encounter the severest resistance.

Even though the federal government has not supplied the leadership which would be so significant and inspiring to the states, there are nonetheless great advances being made by state and city commissions against discrimination. By conciliation and education Negroes and other minority groups have been introduced into employment careers hitherto reserved for whites. How much of this would have occurred without the aid of state action is a matter beyond investigation. But there seems to be consensus among experts in the field of intergroup relations that legal action has been more useful than even some of its advocates could have imagined.

Fair employment laws have not, of course, been enacted in the South with the result that the North, by its insistence on equality in employment, inevitably invites more Negroes to migrate out of the South. The more vigorous the enforcement of a nondiscrimination policy in a particular state, the more likely it seems that such a state will attract more Negroes. Could a strict policy of enforcement lead to an extension of the "problem" of minority races? No indication of such an extension has yet appeared, although it would seem that if there is widespread desegregation in Southern schools a sizable number of Negro teachers hitherto employed in Southern segregated schools may migrate to the North.

In this connection it seems important to note that courts are reluctant to make a finding of bias in employment if there is present some other reasonable explanation for the conduct complained about. For example, a federal court refused to find discrimination in a case brought by eleven Negro teachers whose contracts were not renewed when the public schools of Moberly, Missouri, were integrated in September, 1955. Although 94 of the 98 white teachers received a renewal of contract to teach in the newly integrated school system and all 11 Negro teachers were discharged, the trial judge, sustained on appeal, found no proof of discriminatory abuse of authority on the part of the school board.[36]

Another troublesome but rapidly improving area where bias has

[36] *Brooks* v. *School District of City of Moberly,* 267 F.2d 733. On appeal dismissal was affirmed and the U.S. Supreme Court refused review on Nov. 16, 1959. 4 *Race Relations Law Reporter* 850.

been witnessed is in membership in labor unions. Although some Negro leaders express discontent at the pace at which the AFL-CIO is moving to eliminate both segregated locals and the exclusion of nonwhites from certain craft unions the over-all progress in this matter has been significant. At the present time, however, there is no judicial relief available to Negroes denied membership in a union which has been certified as an exclusive bargaining representative under a federal labor statute.[37] In the 1959 Labor-Management Reporting and Disclosure Act[38] there is a "Bill of Rights" but without a requirement for equality in labor union membership admission.

Despite all the advances in job opportunities made by Negroes since World War II there are still many persons who are not persuaded that law has a significant role to play in promoting the ideal of equal employment opportunities. A clear refutation of this point of view can be seen in the ever-increasing number of Negroes who hold responsible positions with the federal government and with many cities where they serve as policemen and firemen. Where the law insists on equality rapid strides have been witnessed. Where the law is indifferent to equality only "sit-ins" and similar demonstrations can change a deep-seated pattern of bias.

To What Extent Can Law Change Beliefs?

In all the material which has been reviewed on discrimination in housing, education, and employment, the assumption behind the North's new laws proscribing bias in action is that the required change in *conduct* will lead to a change in *belief*. Law, it is assumed, "maintains one set of values against another" to use Dean Roscoe Pound's phrase.[39] By maintaining a set of values the law will supposedly influence public opinion.

The relation of law to public opinion is a complex one. There is solid evidence and impressive authority, however, to support the contention that law is and will continue to be the most powerful force in America in forming the Negro-white relationship. Perhaps it is par-

[37] 5 *Race Relations Law Reporter* 580 (Summer, 1960).
[38] 73 Stat. 519 (1959).
[39] *The Task of Law*, p. 25, by Roscoe Pound, 1944.

ticularly true of this area that in the words of A. V. Dicey, "No facts play a more important part in the creation of opinion than laws themselves."[40]

American Courts, however, have not always been as confident of the power of law as Professor Dicey. "Legislation," according to a Supreme Court 7 to 1 majority in 1896, "is powerless to eradicate racial instincts or to abolish distinctions based on physical differences. . . . If one race be inferior to the other socially, the Constitution of the United States cannot put them upon the same plane."[41] Some twenty years before this decision a 7 to 2 majority was much more affirmative in subscribing to the view that law influences public opinion. In that decision the same Court ruled that a state law excluding Negroes from juries "is practically a brand upon them, affixed by law, an assertion of their inferiority, and *a stimulant to that race prejudice* which is an impediment to securing to individuals of the race that equal justice which the law aims to secure to all others"[42] (emphasis supplied).

While it may be true in the literal sense that the law "is powerless to *eradicate* racial instincts" it seems clear that where an anti-bias law has some support in the community it can inhibit the effects of and even eliminate to some extent the "racial instincts" of its subjects. To what extent and with what rapidity such "instincts" can be eliminated will depend upon the moral climate of the community. In America it will depend more precisely on the fullness of the notion of "equality" as this term is understood by the average citizen. This concept is, of course, the central idea, the principal "fountain of justice" for the American Negro.

The notion of equality is deep in the traditions of the West and in American constitutional and judicial history. The equality of all men was the essence of Cicero's law of nature and of the Stoics' assertion of a universal law for all men. But how much spiritual content does "equality" still contain for the average American? In an age when the moral consensus of society is ambiguous and the public philosophy of the nation is unsupported by mutually agreed-on philosophical prin-

[40] "Lectures on the Relation Between Law and Public Opinion During the Nineteenth Century," p. 138, by A. V. Dicey.
[41] *Plessy* v. *Ferguson*, 163 U.S. 537, 551–552 (1896).
[42] *Strauder* v. *West Virginia*, 100 U.S. 303, 308 (1879).

ciples one can be deeply concerned about the future of the notion of "equality."[43]

It is a truism to state that the concept of human equality has roots in the Catholic tradition deeply grounded in reason and revelation. One can feel, as Maritain and others have affirmed, that the Christian truth of human brotherhood is the ultimate basis of democratic government. Does it not follow therefore that Catholics have a particular mission in the next generation to redefine and deepen the concept of equality which is the basis for all laws forbidding discrimination in housing, education, and employment? It may be that Catholics by reason of their heritage have, in God's Providence, more to contribute to the future welfare of Northern Negroes than any other group in America.

CONCLUSIONS

It is not an overstatement to say that the expected increase of the Negro population in the North during the sixties to some fifteen million presents to the Catholic Church one of the most important challenges it has ever confronted in American history. Catholics among the nation's Negroes number slightly more than 600,000, and about one-third of these reside in Louisiana. The vision of Catholicism and the image of the Church has seemingly not attracted the Negro to any substantial degree. Would the Negro be attracted to the Church if he saw there an organization devoted with all its vast resources to obtaining temporal justice for his people? The answer is, of course, in the affirmative—supposing an infusion of grace from the Holy Spirit on these descendants of African people about whose spiritual destiny Pius XII in 1939 reminded America in tender words in his encyclical *Sertum Laetitiae.*

It is not suggested, of course, that Catholics should be devoted to the temporal welfare of Negroes simply *in order* to attract them to the Church. But an ardent desire to achieve social justice for Negroes and all minorities would be an inevitable sentiment in the hearts of Catholics fully aware of the meaning of human equality and man's Redemption. Well informed and devout Catholics would be in the

[43] For an excellent volume on the notion of equality see *The Quest for Equality,* by Robert J. Harris, Louisiana State University Press, 1960.

very nature of things the leaders in a movement to bring about equality in housing, education, and employment for Negroes.

How many such "well informed and devout Catholics" will emerge in the next decade—an era in which the entire pattern of Northern Negro attitudes will be formed and fashioned for the foreseeable future? At the present time Catholics are seriously underrepresented in most of the intergroup organizations and movements which are working for civic and social equality for Negroes and other minorities. The thrust of Catholic teaching and tradition, coupled with the presence of an ever larger number of America's most mistreated citizens in Northern cities could, with the inspiration of the Holy Spirit, produce that universal flame of indignation which could destroy our cities' ghettoes, wipe out segregation in education, and bring about total equality in employment.

It is time that the Catholics of America fully comprehend the meaning of the words of New Orleans Archbishop Joseph Francis Rummel:

Enforced racial discrimination inflicts incalculable mental and emotional cruelty and pain . . . upon . . . millions of our fellow citizens.

Predictive and Practical Generalizations About Desegregation[1]

JOSEPH H. FICHTER

One of the paradoxes of the American sociocultural system is that change itself has become patterned. Behavior patterns had earlier been considered, even by social scientists, as the rigid, stable, immutable mores, about which William Graham Sumner wrote so determinedly.[2] During the last quarter-century, however, the surging, dynamic American society has witnessed so many innovations that the ordinary observer may conclude that nothing cultural is fixed and

[1] This is an expanded version of a paper delivered at the convention of the American Sociological Association at New York City in August, 1960.

[2] Myrdal's critique of the concept mores is worth rereading in the present context. See his Appendix 1 and 2 in *An American Dilemma* (New York: Harpers, 1944), especially pp. 1031–1032 and 1053–1054.

frozen. Our behavioral expectations have "loosened," but at the same time the expectation of change has become almost fixed. This does not dispense with mores and other patterns; it simply gives most Americans a different mind-set about the viability of the culture.

This concept of social change is central to the propositions discussed here, but its application differs from one institution to another, and in the Southeastern region as compared to the rest of the nation.[3] The desegregation of institutionalized ways of behaving between the races is one of the major shifts of social conduct in the United States,[4] but here too the difference in the Southeast is crucial. The extent and the direction of the ways in which people anticipate the change from a segregated to an integrated society constitute a "predictive generalization." More technically, a predictive generalization is a hypothesis that supposes that a given course of behavior will be followed by a necessary conclusion. A practical generalization is a factual statement about behavior that has actually occurred.

It would be scientifically satisfying if one could assume that the predictive hypothesis is based always on social facts and on a dispassionate knowledge of social trends.[5] Seldom does this appear to be the case. The majority of social scientists are privately steeped in egalitarian values, and their scientific predictions almost necessarily reflect these values. Subconsciously, at least, they seem to "hope for" the removal of discriminatory racial segregation. Their published utterances, however, as Coleman has shown, are couched in almost rigidly cautious terms.[6] These are not the predictions that are here of immediate concern.

[3] H. G. Barnett, *Innovation* (New York: McGraw-Hill, 1953), p. 56, shows that even among Americans these expectations are selective, anticipating less change in religion and family than in technology and art. This "selectivity" must also be applied to the desegregation process.

[4] For an excellent description of these shifts before the Supreme Court decision, see Kenneth Clark, "Desegregation: An Appraisal of the Evidence," *Journal of Social Issues*, vol. 9, No. 4 (1953), 1–77. For a more recent appraisal see James Allen Moss, "Currents of Change in American Race Relations," *The British Journal of Sociology*, vol. 11, No. 3 (Sept., 1960), 232–243.

[5] Almost every introductory textbook in sociology deals with this question of predictability in relation to planning. See, for example, John F. Cuber, *Sociology: A Synopsis of Principles* (New York: Appleton-Century-Crofts, 1955), pp. 14–17; also George A. Lundberg *et al.*, *Sociology* (New York: Harper & Brothers, 1958), p. 79.

[6] A. Lee Coleman, "Social Scientists' Predictions About Desegregation, 1950–1955," *Social Forces*, vol. 38, No. 3 (March, 1960), 258–262, describes predictions found in ten articles and books by eight authors.

This attitudinal bias is quite open and obvious in progressive liberals who are not social scientists. For example, Lillian Smith, an almost ardent advocate of desegregation, made an optimistic prediction in a commencement address at Kentucky State College in June, 1951. She said that the Southern legal institution of segregation would disappear in ten years, and that all graduate schools and undergraduate colleges in the South would be open to Negroes in five years.[7] Her hopeful supposition seems to have been that what was then happening as a desegregation process in the military services would happen at relatively the same rate of speed in all other institutions of the regional subculture.

The case for caution is even stronger when one listens to the people who make pessimistic predictions. This is one of the fascinating repetitive patterns of "traditionalists" in relation to social change and reform. Even where their dire predictions ("it will do more harm than good") do not come true—and they seldom do—this type of person uses precisely the same kind of predictive and pessimistic argument when a program of further social reform is proposed.[8] This is probably why negativism is a generalizing and free-floating attitude, focusing upon changes not only in race relations, but in political, economic, recreational, and other practices. The person who predicts "trouble" in any proposed alterations of the segregation pattern tends also to resist religious and educational and other kinds of changes.

Before analyzing the more pertinent modern examples of contrast between predictive and practical generalizations, we may profitably view some important historical instances. In the earlier decades of this century, when the scientific focus of race was more on biology than on culture, the supposition was that Negro inferiority is innate. The scientific importance of environmental influences simply was not known.[9] The result was that predictions concerning race relations followed two general lines: if the Negro were left to himself he would

[7] Lillian Smith, "Ten Years from Today," *Vital Speeches,* vol. 17, No. 12 (Aug. 15, 1951), 669–672.

[8] See Joseph H. Fichter, *Sociology* (Chicago: University of Chicago Press, 1957), chap. 15, "Change," and chap. 16, "Social Control."

[9] The furious assaults made by racists against the U.S. Supreme Court for its dependence on scientific psychological and sociological findings in *Brown* vs. *Board of Education* have to be explained more on the basis of prejudice than of ignorance. By 1954, the environmental factors had been thoroughly tested and proved.

revert to barbarism and eventually become extinct; if he mingled with the Caucasian his "black blood" would swamp and deteriorate the civilized race. In 1904 William B. Smith predicted the extinction of the white race; and in 1920 Lothrop Stoddard predicted imminent danger to the white stock, first from Asiatic blood, then from Negro blood.[10]

More recently, in 1945, Stuart Landry opposed biological amalgamation of the races in a more sophisticated way. He said that the American Negroes "must remain a separate race and they can achieve success, seek happiness and fulfill their destiny in some other way." He believed that Negroes could obtain economic justice in only three ways: by emigrating from this country, by intensive segregation within this country, or by developing a "parallel civilization" in the United States.[11] Marcus Garvey not only opposed amalgamation of the races but predicted, and worked for, an exalted African Empire to which American Negroes would flock.[12] Even William Du Bois, Garvey's archenemy, was opposed to racial intermarriage and miscegenation, and favorably looked forward to a separate American Negro cultural system.[13]

In many instances the predictions concerning racial amalgamation in America have a double implication: the first is that it will occur; the second is that the race problem will not be solved unless it does occur. Everyone who has studied the question is familiar with the popular lecture that the anthropologist, Ralph Linton, used to deliver on "The Vanishing American Negro," in which he argued that in two centuries our descendants would wonder why we were so disturbed in our time about the race problem.[14] The Negroes would be ab-

[10] William B. Smith, *The Color Line* (New York: McClure, 1904), chap. 5, "A Dip Into the Future"; also Lothrop Stoddard, *The Rising Tide of Color* (New York: Scribners, 1920), chap. 12, "The Crisis of the Ages."

[11] See Stuart Omer Landry, *The Cult of Equality* (New Orleans: Pelican Press, 1945). It would be futile to review the mass of distorted racist "literature" that has been flooding the country more or less surreptitiously during the last five years. Its central and fearful prediction is miscegenation.

[12] For a concise description of the Garvey Movement, see Gunnar Myrdal, *An American Dilemma* (New York: Harper & Brothers, 1944), pp. 746–749.

[13] The most recent analysis of the work of Du Bois is Elliot M. Rudwick, *W. E. B. Du Bois* (Philadelphia: University of Pennsylvania Press, 1960).

[14] Ralph Linton, "The Vanishing American Negro," *American Mercury,* vol. 64, No. 278 (Feb. 1947), 133–139.

sorbed into the white race by the continued contribution of Caucasian genetic characteristics, a process that has been going on since the first importation of Negroes to America. Linton's cultural arguments may still have validity, but his predictions based on biological trends seem to have been demolished by Glass and Li, who maintain that in each generation only 3.6 per cent of all the genes of North American Negroes are freshly introduced from North American whites. Their prediction is that "complete mixing of the white and Negro races in the United States will probably take from 1,000 to 2,000 years, or forty to seventy generations."[15]

The notion that only biological amalgamation would solve the American race problem is a fatalistic prediction that negates the accumulated scientific knowledge of cultural pluralism. No less a person than Franz Boas published a prediction to the effect that the problem of American race relations would not be solved until the Negro is no longer recognizable, that is, until he has been absorbed by the white race.[16] Historical evidence points clearly in the opposite direction. The greatest amount of miscegenation occurred when the Negroes were held in the greatest inferiority of slavery. As the Negroes have moved toward equality the amount of biological mixing has steadily decreased.[17] This need not constitute a unilinear trend for the future, but it does tend to destroy the current predictions of racial "purists" who oppose social equality because it will "inevitably" lead to intermarriage.[18]

Since the theory of innate inferiority of Negroes has been thor-

[15] See the report of Bentley Glass and C. C. Li in *Science News Letter,* vol. 62, No. 12 (Sept. 20, 1952) 189. Myrdal, *op. cit.,* pp. 132–136, states confidently, after reviewing the factors involved, that "there are no reasons to believe that a more complete amalgamation between whites and Negros will occur within the surveyable future" (p. 136).

[16] Franz Boas, *Race and Democratic Society* (New York: Augustine, 1945).

[17] The historical facts are known, but the connection between them is not recognized in the current defense ideology of Southeasterners. An example is William D. Workman, Jr., *The Case for the South* (New York, Devin-Adair, 1959), chap. 11, "Mixing the Races," who states the historical fact of decreasing miscegenation, but *predicts* that it will increase.

[18] See the calm and critical evaluation of this "opportunistic rationalization" by Gunnar Myrdal, *op. cit.,* pp. 589–592; also Randall Risdom, "A Study of Interracial Marriages," *Sociology and Social Research,* vol. 39, (Nov.–Dec., 1954), 92–95; and Joseph Golden, "Social Control of Negro-White Intermarriage," *Social Forces,* vol. 36, No. 3 (March, 1958), 267–269.

oughly discredited,[19] and since the hypothesis concerning the biological amalgamation of the races will not be proved or disproved in our day, let us turn to some of the more manageable predictions that have been made concerning the factors and variables in the desegregation process. We may look briefly at six of these predictive generalizations, which are as follows: (*a*) industrialization and labor unions would improve race relations; (*b*) whites are more willing to give Negroes economic opportunities than to make other concessions; (*c*) bloodshed and violence will accompany every attempted change in Southern race relations; (*d*) the removal of segregation cannot be successfully legislated; (*e*) Negroes cannot make progress without the sympathetic help of the "better white people"; (*f*) gradualism is the only effective approach to desegregation.

(*a*) One of the most optimistic of these predictive generalizations held that growing industry and stronger labor unions in the South would necessarily and almost "automatically" improve race relations and hasten desegregation. This is a rational hypothesis based upon the assumption that hiring and upgrading in industry are impersonal and functional, and that the organized labor movement deplores discrimination from motives of self-interest and democracy. Yinger and Simpson have theorized along these lines with the beguiling question, "Can Segregation Survive in an Industrial Society?"[20] The answer is, of course, a resounding affirmative. Nicholls remarks that "Few Southerners have yet faced up to the question of whether they want industrialization bad[ly] enough to give up firmly held Southern traditions which are inconsistent with it."[21]

Everyone knows that right after the war the CIO failed in its famed

[19] Professor Henry E. Garrett has not yet bowed to the evidence. In the Foreword to Audrey M. Shuey, *The Testing of Negro Intelligence* (New York, Bell, 1958) he points out that although some Negroes score above the white medians, the mean differences between the races still persist, and "the regularity and constancy of the results strongly imply a racial basis for these differences." See also the popular article by Frank C. J. McGurk, "A Scientist's Report on Race Differences," *U.S. News & World Report* (Sept. 21, 1956), 92–96; and the rebuttal of this article by a large group of social scientists, as reported in *The New York Times* for Oct. 16, 1956, p. 14.

[20] J. Milton Yinger and George E. Simpson, *The Antioch Review*, vol. 18, No. 1 (March, 1958), 15–24, make a notable understatement: "The obstacles to the inclusion of Negroes in labor unions in the South must not be minimized."

[21] William H. Nicholls, *Southern Tradition and Regional Progress* (Chapel Hill: University of North Carolina Press, 1960), p. 155.

"Operation Dixie," and that the 1956 AFL-CIO drive for membership in the South was anything but successful. Southern members of organized labor are fully represented in the White Citizens Councils of the various states. Every time the national officers of the union venture a pronouncement in favor of racial equality they hear rumblings of labor secession among the Southern locals. The result is that the labor unions (like the professional groups of teachers, lawyers, physicians, nurses, and others) continue to countenance separate locals for Negroes and whites.[22]

Manufacturing plants in the South are not "automatically" absorbing Negroes into their work force, much less giving them equal job opportunities, in spite of a few exceptions like the International Harvester Company.[23] Management people privately argue that they are in business for profit, and not for social reform. Yet some companies have successfully used the integration issue in their propaganda against unions. They perpetuate the weakness of the labor movement by stressing the dreaded "social equality" that would eventuate from biracial unions.

(*b*) A second prediction is closely allied to this, and it forms a part of Myrdal's oft-repeated "rank order of discrimination."[24] According to this hypothesis, white people in the South are more willing to grant economic opportunities to Negroes than they are to make other concessions to them. This does not suggest opportunities for Negroes equal to those of whites, as is evidenced from the fact that during the 1957–1958 recession in areas where one out of fifteen white workers were unemployed, one out of seven Negroes were also out of jobs.

---

[22] "The history of Texas labor has been one in which Negroes have been unionized in negligible numbers, segregated in colored unions, and discriminated against by white unions." This is the problem of "membership pressures." See Murray E. Polakoff, "Internal Pressures on the Texas State CIO Council, 1937–1955," *Industrial and Labor Relations Review*, vol. 12, No. 2 (Jan., 1959), 227–242.

[23] See John Hope, "Industrial Integration of Negroes: The Upgrading Process," *Human Organization*, vol. 11, No. 4 (1952), 5–14; also Robert Weintraub, "Employment Integration and Racial Wage Differences in a Southern Plant," *Industrial and Labor Relations Review*, vol. 12, No. 2 (Jan., 1959), 214–226. Outside the Southeast there are undoubted advances in Negro industrial opportunities. See, for example, Jack London and Richard Hammett, "Impact of Company Policy Upon Discrimination," *Sociology and Social Research*, vol. 39 (Sept.–Oct., 1954), 88–91.

[24] Gunnar Myrdal, *op. cit.* pp. 60–67.

There is ample evidence that in the South even the federal government agencies (with the exception of the Post Offices in the larger cities) are not carrying out their much publicized Fair Employment Practices. The same failure of employment justice is seen in the companies and industries with government contracts that stipulate fair employment.[25]

There is a curious kind of economic irrationality at work here. The segregated system—if facilities were equal—would be prohibitively costly. Many observers have agreed that this tremendous expense is "one of the strongest arguments against a continuance of the separate but equal system."[26] This argument has never been tested because fully equal facilities have nowhere been provided in the Southeast, but there is a strong present trend to indicate that convinced racists are willing to pay the cost of equal facilities, if forced to do so, rather than suffer the humiliation of desegregation. Municipal, county, and state administrations have made a small start in the gigantic task of "bringing up" public facilities for Negroes, but no one realistically expects that the economically underprivileged Southeast can accomplish this task.

On the other hand, Oliver Cromwell Cox's thesis that capitalist exploitation is basic to racial discrimination seems to be valid in the Southeast.[27] Resistance to economic equality is apparently much stronger than the prophets had anticipated. The general wage rate in the Southeast has risen, and Negroes have benefited from it, but

[25] That FEPC is effective, as well as SCAD in New York State, is shown by James Rorty, "FEPC in the States: A Progress Report," *The Antioch Review*, vol. 18, No. 3 (Fall, 1958), 317–329, who quotes Elmer Carter: "The dire and forbidden prophecies of the consequences of the enactment have not been realized" (326).

[26] Ambrose Caliver, "Segregation in American Education: An Overview," *Annals of the American Academy of Political and Social Science*, vol. 304 (March, 1956), 17–25.

[27] Oliver Cromwell Cox, *Caste, Class and Race* (New York: Doubleday, 1948) deals also with the paradox that racial discrimination is lower in the Northeast where capitalism is furthest advanced (p. 569). The strongest intellectual criticism of Myrdal's work has come from the Marxist camp. Cox, pp. 509–538, calls Myrdal's "A Mystical Approach," and Herbert Aptheker's booklet, *The Negro People in America* (New York: International Publishers, 1946), criticizes his factual data. It is a curious sidelight on propaganda that the Southern politicians and racists, who put the "Communist" label on Myrdal, do not seem to recognize their own Marxist allies.

studies of unemployment areas show that Negroes are still the poorest paid, the last hired, and the first fired.[28] Negro domestics are now being better paid only because the supply of this kind of worker is beginning to run short of the demand. But economic pressure is still the sure weapon in the fight against desegregation. The White Citizens Councils boldly advocate and apply economic penalties on Negroes who seek voting rights, better housing, schooling, and other facilities.

(c) A third and very widespread prediction was that bloodshed and violence would accompany every attempted improvement in Southern race relations. The brave assertions were that the South would fight rather than desegregate, that there would not be enough federal prisons to hold the Southern dissenters. Virginius Dabney predicted in January, 1943, that agitators and rabble-rousers were pushing the country toward "an interracial explosion which may make the race riots of the First World War and its aftermath seem mild by comparison." He feared that "hundreds if not thousands," would be killed. Mark Ethridge claimed that "there is no power in the world—not even in all the mechanized armies of the earth, Allied and Axis— which could now force Southern white people to the abandonment of the principles of social desegregation."[29]

To what extent are these predictions being realized at the present time? Violence and "disturbances" have always been characteristic of the Southeast, where crimes against the person show the highest rates in the country. Recently the floodlights of national, and even international, publicity have been focused on the hundred-odd nighttime bombings of schools, synagogues, and homes, and on murders like those of Lamar Smith, Emmet Till, and Clinton Melton in Mississippi. These may well be called examples of "normal" Southern white

[28] See Gary S. Becker, *The Economics of Discrimination* (Chicago: University of Chicago Press, 1957), chaps. 7, 8, "Discrimination Against Non-Whites"; also the research report on case studies in various parts of the South, *Selected Studies of Negro Employment in the South* (Washington: National Planning Association, 1955).

[29] These and similar dire warnings are quoted by C. Vann Woodward, *The Strange Career of Jim Crow* (New York: Oxford, 1955), p. 106. Also during World War II an article in *The Christian Century*, vol. 62 (March 21, 1945), predicted that "with each Negro gain, racial antagonism is likely to increase. Unless forces of reconciliation not now visible quickly appear in strength, strikes, riots and bloodshed may be expected to recur."

violence, and not a new outburst against the new threat of desegregation.[30]

The forming of mobs in Little Rock, Jacksonville, Biloxi, New Orleans, and elsewhere, were certainly expressions of resistance by whites to various forms of desegregation. Since mobs are typically cowardly, however, there were no instances of individual "bravery" except perhaps that of the lone civilian who tried to take a gun from a soldier in Little Rock. No serious race riots "Northern style" have occurred since the Second World War,[31] and the organized forays of whites into Negro neighborhoods, which were the "Southern style" of one-sided race riots, have also been sharply on the decline in the same period.[32]

It must be noted that the prediction of violence was a more or less hidden threat by whites, and not a fear that Negroes would retaliate after a long history of injusice. The careful, legal steps of the NAACP, and the orderly, passive resistance of the Martin King movement seem to be providing a subconscious moral lesson to all but the extreme racists. Guy Johnson's remark in 1954, after surveying the previous five years, seems applicable to the ensuing five years. "Despite numerous predictions of violence," he wrote, "the transition to racial co-education in southern universities has been accomplished without a single serious incident of friction."[33] A litany of cases can be cited of desegregation in street transportation, libraries, parks, golf courses, schools and colleges, where little trouble occurred and no blood was shed.

(d) A fourth traditional prediction is that "you can't legislate morality," which in this case means that law is not an effective instrument to remove patterns of discrimination and segregation. This tradition goes back to the strength of Sumner's mores; and even social scientists, until recently, appeared to be reluctant to relinquish this

[30] This is obviously in disagreement with the racist interpretation which holds that "things were going fine till the Supreme Court started all this trouble." See John Bartlow Martin, *The Deep South Says Never* (New York: Ballantine, 1957).

[31] See Allen D. Grimshaw, "Urban Racial Violence in the United States," *The American Journal of Sociology*, vol. 66, No. 2 (Sept., 1960), 109–119.

[32] Writers like Harry Ashmore, *An Epitaph for Dixie* (New York: Norton, 1957), and William Peters: *The Southern Temper* (New York, Doubleday, 1959), agree that the racists' resort to violence is on the decline.

[33] Guy B. Johnson, "A Sociologist Looks at Racial Desegregation in the South," *Social Forces*, vol. 33 (1954), 1–10.

hypothesis. The man on the street, and particularly the white Southerner, still tends to cite the failure of the Volstead Act as proof that law cannot change custom. Of all the predictive generalizations discussed here, this one has been the most completely contradicted—yet it continues to be expressed with great vehemence.[34]

The dilatory and gentle manner in which the federal judges have seen to the application of the U.S. Supreme Court decision of 1954 does not negate the fact that this kind of prediction is now untenable. The fact is that every substantial improvement gained by American Negroes during the past two decades has been made through the legislative and judicial processes.[35] As Peters remarks, "every evidence of significant progress on the long road to equality has come about, directly or indirectly, as a result of legal coercion or the threat of it."[36] Even the Montgomery bus boycott, which looked like a victory for massive and passive resistance, was really and ultimately settled by a court order. It was the genius of Thurgood Marshall and the NAACP that they did not allow themselves to be distracted into any other than the orderly, legal approach.

No other mechanism has been so effective as the law and the courts in the process of desegregation. The strongest proof that custom and mores are likely to weaken before the onslaught of law is found in the almost frantic attempts of the legislatures of Southern states to use the same legal instruments to offset the effect of the Constitution and federal legislation. Hundreds of new laws have been introduced in Southern states since 1954 to preserve the Southern white "way of life."[37] It seems significant in this connection that the dominant leadership among American Negroes is switching from

[34] See the criticisms of Arnold M. Rose, "Sociological Factors in the Effectiveness of Projected Legislative Remedies," *Journal of Legal Education,* vol. 11, No. 4 (1959), 470–481.

[35] The history of the restrictive covenant in housing is an excellent example of this. See Clement E. Vose, *Caucasians Only* (Berkeley: University of California Press, 1959).

[36] William Peters, *The Southern Temper* (New York, Doubleday, 1959), p. 275. Note also the observations of Harry S. Ashmore, *The Other Side of Jordan,* (New York, Norton, 1960), chap. 10, "The Uses of Law," dealing with legal progress outside the Southeastern states. See also The Symposium in the *Notre Dame Lawyer,* vol. 34, No. 5 (1959), whole issue.

[37] See, for example, Walter F. Murphy, "The South Counterattacks: The Anti-NAACP Laws," *Western Political Quarterly,* vol. 12, No. 2 (June, 1959), 371–390.

ministers of religion to legal experts. This legal emphasis, effective though it is, is probably regretted by many Americans who would prefer that education, or religion, or economic rationality should be the most potent force in the improvement of race relations.

(e) A fifth prediction, shared in the past and often repeated by both whites and Negroes, is that Negroes cannot make progress toward desegregation without the sympathetic cooperation of the better white people. In the long run it is probably true to say that increasing tolerance of the great majority of white Americans is an essential factor in Negro progress. In this sense, the climate of national liberal opinion has shifted strongly since the war, but it has not moved fast enough in the South. Negroes have grown increasingly impatient, particularly in the South, with the slowness of white benignity. In practically all major current instances of improvement Negroes have themselves taken the initiative. Proper credit must be given to President Roosevelt for his executive order concerning fair employment in war industries, but it is sometimes forgotten that A. Philip Randolph's proposal for a Negro march on Washington was a strong incentive for that order.[38] In this and other ways organized Negroes now address themselves to the whole nation, rather than to a few white friends and leaders.

Martin Luther King, in his book *Stride Toward Freedom*, indicates that begging from the white folks, and depending upon their good friends among the whites are no longer acceptable Negro strategies.[39] There seems to be an analogy here too when one considers the politically appointed administrations of Negro Southern colleges vis à vis the student sit-ins. It was in clear defiance of their educational elders that most of these sit-ins occurred in the cafeterias and drugstores of Southern cities. This threat to the status of older leaders (many of whom had long depended on white cooperation) was recognized at the 1960 convention of the NAACP. The delegates hastened to pledge

[38] Randolph called for ten thousand "black Americans" to march on Washington. "We shall not call upon our white friends to march with us. There are some things Negroes must do alone." The President issued the executive order on June 25, 1941, a week before the march on Washington was to take place, and on July 19 appointed the first FEPC. See Herbert Garfinkel, *When Negroes March* (Glencoe: The Free Press, 1959).

[39] Martin Luther King, *Stride Toward Freedom* (New York: Harper & Brothers, 1958).

full support to the college students who promote the sit-in and kneel-in demonstrations.

It may also be said in this connection that some of the sociological assumptions concerning the community power structure seem to have gone awry. The informal groups of white people, like HOPE and SOS, who organized to keep the public schools open in Virginia, in Atlanta, and in New Orleans, have found that the "power people" in local politics and business are the least effective and the most fearful in this situation. Some of them have long protested that they are "the best friends the Negroes ever had," but it now appears that their "friendship" has more often been a brake on Negro aspirations. Whatever their reasons for reluctance, most of them shy away from any commitment to keep the public schools open—and desegregated.[40]

(f) Although there are probably many others, we might mention here a sixth and final prediction that seems to have misfired. This is the notion that gradualism is the only effective approach to racial desegregation. As a short-range, immediate strategy of conciliation and expediency, it may have been acceptable by Negroes in the days of Booker T. Washington. The compulsion to follow a gradualistic approach in practice does not mean the acceptance of gradualism as a policy, yet the warnings that "this is going to take a long, long, time" are still being issued by white liberals.

The brief history of military desegregation has become the classic refutation of those who do believe in the necessity of the gradual process.[41] It began in 1950 with the report of the Fahy Committee and it was practically completed in 1955. Scientific studies of the armed forces have shown invariably that the removal of segregation was accompanied by increased efficiency and by decreased friction and tension between the races.[42] Obviously, the percentage of Negroes at each level of the military does not match the percentage of Negroes

[40] This seems to be true even of the white community leaders studied in North Carolina by Melvin M. Tumin, *Desegregation: Resistance and Readiness* (Princeton: Princeton University Press, 1958), chap. 10, "The Quality and Role of Leaders in the Process of Desegregation."

[41] Kenneth Clark, *op. cit.*, pp. 34–48, includes the U.S. Navy among his factual examples of gradual desegregation.

[42] See Robert J. Dwyer, "The Negro in the U.S. Army," *Sociology and Social Research*, vol. 38 (1953), 103–112. The successful desegregation of major league baseball is perhaps a more dramatic example of rapid change since the "authoritative" factor of the military was not at work here.

in the total American population, but this is not at all the implication of total desegregation.[43] At any rate, the military experience indicates clearly that intelligent planning and competent administration can short-cut the gradualist notion that "time will take care of the problem."

The fact that in many areas the process of desegregation has been slowed down by a variety of delaying tactics does not mean that a long transitional period was either necessary or desirable. There are those who now believe that much animosity and suffering could have been avoided if the United States Supreme Court had declared that— instead of "all deliberate speed"—the first minimum steps toward school desegregation would have to take place in September of 1954. The gradualistic approach can be questioned both as a legal precedent and as a moral principle, and seems to lack logical support in either case.[44] As a strategy for the practical removal of segregation, it is at this point of time an obvious failure.

There has been no intention in this discussion to indict social science for an inability to predict human conduct. The fact is, of course, that standardization of conduct and of behavioral norms is essential to an on-going social order, and where there is order there is predictability. In the case of racial desegregation in the Southeastern region, attempts at prediction are complicated by the attitudinal values of the observer, to a small extent among social scientists, to a very large extent among lay observers. The greater problem, however, lies outside the observer, because the "old order" must necessarily change to a new order (with different cultural norms and patterns) as racial desegregation becomes a reality.

In his article, which listed specific predictions by social scientists about desegregation, Coleman pointed out three "constant" determinants. The first two are (*a*) the institutionalized racial dualism of the South, and (*b*) the norms of racial superiority held by the whites

[43] James G. Evans and David A. Lane, Jr., "Integration in the Armed Services," *Annals of the American Academy of Political and Social Science*, vol. 304 (1956), 78–85.

[44] It must be remembered that the topic discussed here is racial desegregation at this particular point of history. The alternatives are not "sudden" and "revolutionary," nor do they refer to all other social and cultural change. See the remarks of Emory S. Bogardus, "Gradualism as a Concept," *Sociology and Social Research*, vol. 44 (Nev.–Dec., 1959), 119–124.

in the South. Against these, though vaguely subscribed to by many Southerners, is (*c*) the American ideology of human equality.[45] The problem of prediction was then complicated with a long list of "variables" or conditions under which the constant determinants were expected to function. The predictions themselves then tended to become long-range and generalized forecasts of changes that would most likely occur. For this reason one can evaluate only vaguely the extent to which they have "proved out."

When culture norms are stable the prediction of social conduct can be fairly accurate. In the Southeast the norms governing the relations between the races contain two elements of instability: they differ sharply from those of the American culture, and they are now constantly under challenge to change. The examples of erroneous predictions that we have discussed here trace their basic fallacy to a neglect of these two elements. It has been a normal assumption that the lawlessness of the Southeast would continue into the future, and thus promote bloodshed and negate legal processes when racial desegregation is attempted. Since the Southeast has been a slow-moving subculture with a caste system, the assumption was made that desegregation must be a gradual process dependent for its success on the kindly paternalism of the upper-class people in the white caste. The economic and industrial assumptions are, in a sense, "imports" to this regional problem. They emerge from the total American culture, where they tend to be effective, and not from the Southeastern subculture, where they are resisted to the extent that they are recognized as potential factors for improved race relations.

There is a strong temptation to conclude a discussion of this kind by making one's own predictions about the future of racial desegregation in the South. The temptation can be overcome by substituting the final footnote of an article written in 1946 by Rudolph Heberle, in which he commented upon the South's coming-of-age. "For the benefit of such critics as might object to the use of this metaphoric term because it has a connotation of progress, I would like to point out that some people do not like the idea of 'growing up' at all."[46]

[45] Coleman, *op. cit.*, pp. 258–262. The author himself declines any attempt to evaluate the predictions.

[46] Rudolf Heberle, "A Sociological Interpretation of Social Change in the South," *Social Forces*, vol. 25, No. 1 (Oct., 1946), 9–15.

Psychological Research and Educational Desegregation

ANNE ANASTASI

Psychological problems, facts, and principles have been repeatedly incorporated in discussions of racial segregation and desegregation in the country's schools. One of the most vivid demonstrations of the role played by psychology in this issue is to be found in the statement signed by thirty-five social scientists and submitted to the Supreme Court of the United States in the case which culminated in the momentous decision of May 17, 1954.[1] Findings of psychological research, as well as opinions expressed by psychologists, have likewise

---

[1] Appendix to appellants' briefs: statements by social scientists, *Social Problems*, 1955, 2, 227–235.

been cited in state court proceedings[2] and in articles in the popular press both in support of desegregation[3] and—less frequently—in defense of continued segregation.[4]

Within psychology itself, several areas of research have important implications for educational desegregation. Social psychology provides information on the nature and development of racial attitudes, prejudices, and stereotypes, as well as on their influence upon intergroup behavior. Observations of clinical and child psychologists point up the effects of segregation upon personality development. And differential psychology is concerned with the fundamental question of the extent and origins of group differences in aptitudes, achievement, and personality characteristics. Some of the most relevant findings in these different areas will be examined in the following sections.

RACIAL ATTITUDES AND GROUP RELATIONS

One of the problems connected with desegregation in the schools— or in any other aspect of community life—centers around the attitudes of the two groups toward each other. Whether the transition from segregated to integrated facilities occurs smoothly and without "incidents" or whether it is accompanied by hostility, violence, and disruption of normal functions depends at least in part upon existing community attitudes and their susceptibility to change under various conditions. A considerable body of psychological data bearing upon these questions is now available.[5] It is generally recognized by social psychologists, for example, that group prejudices and hostility toward members of minority groups are not "natural" or "innate." Racial attitudes are learned by the individual as he grows up in a community that already displays such attitudes. The child assimilates the prej-

[2] E.g., *Brown* v. *Board of Education,* Kansas, 98 F. Supp. 797; *Davis* v. *County School Board,* Virginia, 103 F. Supp. 337.

[3] E.g., Various, "Does Race Really Make a Difference in Intelligence?", *U.S. News & World Report,* Oct. 26, 1956, 74–76.

[4] F. C. J. McGurk, "Psychological Tests—a Scientist's Report on Race Differences," *U.S. News & World Report,* Sept. 21, 1956, 92–96.

[5] G. W. Allport, *The Nature of Prejudice* (Cambridge, Mass.: Addison-Wesley, 1954); S. W. Cook, "Desegregation: A Psychological Analysis," *American Psychologist,* 1957, 12, 1–13; O. Klineberg, *Social Psychology* (rev. ed.; New York: Holt, 1954), Ch. 19; G. Saenger, *The Social Psychology of Prejudice* (New York: Harper & Brothers, 1953); M. and Carolyn W. Sherif, *An Outline of Social Psychology* (rev. ed.; New York: Harper & Brothers, 1956), Ch. 16 and 19.

udices and stereotypes of his group early in life. Thus studies at the preschool level have revealed clearly developed racial attitudes among both white and Negro children reared in communities in which racial discrimination prevailed.[6] By the time he reaches high school age, the individual has usually forgotten the role that parents, teachers, and other associates played in the transmission of social norms and comes to believe that his attitudes represent his immediate, personal reaction, which he may rationalize in a variety of ways.[7]

There is evidence, moreover, that such attitudes are acquired much oftener through assimilation of existing social norms than through contacts with members of other groups. Thus individuals manifest as much prejudice toward groups with which they have had no contact, but about which stereotypes are current in the community, as they do toward groups with which they have personally interacted. On the other hand, it cannot be assumed that increasing contact will always improve intergroup attitudes and reduce prejudice.[8] In any discussion of the effect of contact upon attitude changes, it is necessary to define in more specific terms both the conditions under which association occurs and the characteristics of the individuals who are in contact.

Members of two groups may encounter one another daily, but with little opportunity to become acquainted, as in the case of a Negro elevator operator and white passengers who ride the elevator to their offices. A situation in which members of the two races work together toward the achievement of a common goal on a job or in a community project illustrates the other extreme. Also relevant is the relative status of the participants in the contact situation. It is apparent, for example, that the presence of Negroes in menial positions would have a very different effect from that of Negro co-workers or supervisors. Similarly, background characteristics of the persons who come together will

[6] K. B. and Mamie K. Clark, "Skin Color as a Factor in Racial Identification of Negro Preschool Children," *Journal of Social Psychology*, 1940, 11, 159–169; K. B. and Mamie K. Clark, "Racial Identification and Preference in Negro Children," in T. M. Newcomb and E. L. Hartley (eds.), *Readings in Social Psychology* (New York: Holt, 1947); Mary E. Goodman, *Race Awareness in Young Children* (Cambridge, Mass.: Addison-Wesley, 1952).

[7] E. L. and Ruth E. Horowitz, "Development of Social Attitudes in Children," *Sociometry*, 1937–1938, 1, 301–338.

[8] G. W. Allport, *op. cit.;* S. W. Cook, article cited; G. Saenger, *op. cit.;* M. and Carolyn W. Sherif, *op. cit.*

determine the extent and direction of resulting attitude shifts. If one encounters predominantly Negroes from the lowest socioeconomic and educational levels, the experience may serve only to heighten prevailing stereotypes. Contact between Negroes and whites whose interests, training, and background are more nearly alike would tend to have the reverse effect. The preexisting attitudes of members of both ethnic groups, as well as the social norms of the groups with which they identify, would likewise help to determine what changes, if any, occur from any specific kind of contact.

Relevant data are provided by a recent investigation utilizing observational and interviewing techniques to explore possible sources of interracial tensions and conflicts in a voluntary adolescent interracial group.[9] The data showed that extent of spontaneous personal contact was not a reliable indicator of favorable interracial attitudes. A consideration of the specific emotional needs that motivated such contacts and the preexisting attitudes of both Negro and white subjects provided a basis for understanding the success or failure of interracial activities in the group.

Another type of research finding which has an important bearing upon desegregation problems is that verbally expressed opinions are not necessarily a dependable indicator of actual behavior in contact situations. In interviews with white women in New York City, it was found that individuals who had been seen making purchases from Negro salesgirls denied that they would do so.[10] More directly related to educational desegregation is a study conducted in June, 1954, in Washington, D.C.[11] Interviews of a cross section of the Washington population indicated that 52 per cent of the white respondents believed the Supreme Court decision to be bad, 24 per cent considered it good, and another 24 per cent were neutral. The following fall, the Washington schools were desegregated with no disturbance except one strike by high school students, which collapsed after a few days when it received no support from adult members of the community. When the same investigators reinterviewed the original

[9] I. Katz, *Conflict and Harmony in an Adolescent Interracial Group* (New York: New York University Press, 1955).

[10] G. Saenger, and Emily Gilbert, "Customer Reactions to the Integration of Negro Sales Personnel," *International Journal of Opinion and Attitude Research,* 1950, 4, 57–76.

[11] Cited by S. W. Cook, article cited, p. 2.

sample of respondents toward the end of the school year, they found that even among those who had originally characterized the Supreme Court decision as "bad," 39 per cent felt that desegregation was working "very well" or "fairly well."

It should be noted that the results of research on interracial attitudes are more closely related to techniques of effective implementation than to the basic question of the psychological rationale for desegregation. As far as the latter question is concerned, the major implication of available data on attitudes is that intergroup attitudes *are* modifiable. Hence racial antipathies and expressions of opposition to desegregation do not constitute insurmountable obstacles to successful integration, nor can they serve as serious arguments against desegregation in the schools. Nevertheless, attitudes need to be carefully considered in the choice of specific procedures for effecting educational integration in any particular locality.

EFFECTS OF SEGREGATION UPON PERSONALITY DEVELOPMENT

In its decision of May 17, 1954, the Supreme Court of the United States eliminated legal recognition of the doctrine of "separate but equal facilities" in public education, concluding that "separate educational facilities are inherently unequal." The psychological justification for the latter statement stems largely from the effects of segregation upon the individual's self concept and his personality development. When the Negro school child—or college or professional school student—is subjected to enforced segregation in American schools, such a condition serves as a symbol and constant reminder of an implied inferiority. The mere act of segregation is thus likely to undermine the individual's self-confidence, motivation, and achievement, and to curtail the effective utilization of his abilities. A further educational handicap, of course, is the reduction or elimination of intellectual interaction with members of the more privileged dominant subculture.

Clark[12] has summarized the possible deleterious effects of segrega-

[12] K. B. Clark, "Effect of Prejudice and Discrimination on Personality Development," *Fact-Finding Report, Mid-Century White House Conference on Children and Youth* (Children's Bureau, Federal Security Agency, 1950; mimeographed); *Idem,* "Race Prejudice and Children," *Child,* 1953, 17, 113–115, 117; *Idem, Prejudice and Your Child* (Boston: Beacon Press, 1955).

tion and racial discrimination upon the child's personality development. The minority group child reared under such conditions tends to experience frustration, conflict, feelings of inferiority, and loss of self-respect. The effects of these conditions upon the individual's behavior will vary with other concomitant circumstances, such as the educational and socioeconomic level of his family. Some individuals will turn to overt aggression and hostility toward whites or—where that is too hazardous—toward other Negroes. Such behavior, of course, tends further to strengthen the stereotype of the impulsive, immature, irresponsible Negro. Others may display withdrawn and submissive behavior, with apathy and lack of initiative. A defeatist attitude is a common reaction. Hypersensitivity is likewise a frequent response, the individual perceiving hostility and rejection on the part of his associates even when none exists.

Dollard[13] has suggested that the Negro may assume an attitude of stupidity and lethargy as a defense mechanism against frustration and oppression. This reaction would provide a sort of revenge against the dominant group and would enable the individual to avoid disagreeable responsibilities. Such behavior fits the stereotype of the slow-moving, dull Negro which has been popularized by comedians in movies, radio, and television. Along the same general lines, Brown[14] has argued that the linguistic development of the Negro may be hindered by social pressures that tend to inhibit verbalization. Inarticulateness reduces the possibility of incurring the hostility of the dominant social group, and might thus be "cultivated" as a measure of discretion.

Segregation may also have injurious effects upon the personality development of majority group children. Clark[15] refers to the conflicting attitudes that these children are taught, including racial prejudice and discrimination on the one hand and democratic principles and the brotherhood of man on the other. Such a conflict may lead to guilt feelings, cynicism, rejection of authority, or rigid and un-

[13] J. Dollard, *Caste and Class in a Southern Town* (2nd ed.; New York: Harper & Brothers, 1949).

[14] F. Brown, "An Experimental and Critical Study of the Intelligence of Negro and White Kindergarten Children," *Journal of Genetic Psychology*, 1944, 65, 161–175.

[15] K. B. Clark, *Prejudice and Your Child, op. cit.*

reasoning conformity. Moreover, children who acquire the racial prejudices of their group are being taught to gain personal status and prestige in spurious and unproductive ways. This follows from the fact that "when comparing themselves to members of the minority group, they are not required to evaluate themselves in terms of the more basic standards of actual personal ability and achievement."[16]

That the dominant group child may be adversely affected by racial segregation in the ways mentioned above is suggested by clinical observation and by general psychological knowledge regarding personality development. Owing to the difficulties of carrying out controlled experiments in this area, however, there is a dearth of direct data on this question. The injurious effects of segregation upon minority group members, on the other hand, are more clearly apparent. Relevant information is provided by studies of preschool and school-age children, utilizing observations of spontaneous behavior as well as response to specially designed test situations.[17] Members of the Negro minority group, against which discrimination is practiced, tend to assimilate the cultural stereotypes associated with their race even earlier than do white children of the dominant subculture.[18] From an early age, they learn to think of members of their race as belonging in menial positions and to ascribe inferiority and undesirable traits to them. For example, studies of children at the preschool and primary levels have shown that, when offered white and Negro dolls, the large majority of Negro children preferred the white doll.[19] They

[16] Appendix to appellants' briefs: statements by social scientists, *Social Problems*, 1955, 2, 229.

[17] K. B. and Mamie K. Clark, "Skin Color as a Factor in Racial Identification of Negro Preschool Children," *loc. cit.*; K. B. and Mamie K. Clark, "Racial Identification and Preference in Negro Children," *loc. cit.*; Mary E. Goodman, *op. cit.*; Ruth E. Horowitz, "Racial Aspects of Self-Identification in Nursery School Children," *Journal of Psychology*, 1939, 7, 91–99; Helen L. Koch, "The Social Distance Between Certain Racial, Nationality, and Skin-Pigmentation Groups in Selected Populations of American School Children," *Journal of Genetic Psychology*, 1946, 68, 63–95; Marian Radke-Yarrow, Helen G. Trager, and Hadassah Davis, "Social Perceptions and Attitudes of Children," *Genetic Psychology Monographs*, 1949, 40, 327–477.

[18] K. B. and Mamie C. Clark, "Skin Color as a Factor in Racial Identification of Negro Preschool Children," *loc. cit.*; K. B. and Mamie K. Clark, "Racial Identification and Preference in Negro Children," *loc. cit.*; Mary E. Goodman, *op. cit.*; Ruth E. Horwitz, article cited.

[19] K. B. and Mamie K. Clark, "Racial Identification and Preference in Negro Children," *loc. cit.*; Mary E. Goodman, *op. cit.*

seemed to reject the brown doll more than did the white children, often calling it "dirty" and "ugly," while they described the white doll in such terms as "pretty" and "nice." It should be added, of course, that in the previous experience of both Negro and white children with dolls as such, white dolls undoubtedly predominate. Negro dolls would thus represent a less familiar toy.

Some of the specific personality difficulties that may result from racial prejudice and discrimination are illustrated by case studies of Negro children who were treated at a child guidance center in New York City.[20] Several of these children had migrated from southern communities. Additional relevant data are provided by an investigation of Negro children attending segregated schools in Delaware in 1951.[21] Staff members of a New York clinic examined these children for the explicit purpose of determining the psychological effects of school segregation. Their findings were subsequently submitted to the Delaware courts in connection with a school segregation case. In 1953, following educational desegregation in Delaware, members of the same clinic returned to study twenty-two children, ten of whom had been investigated prior to desegregation. In a published summary of results,[22] it is reported that, after desegregation, the Negro children improved conspicuously in their schoolwork, not only because of superior facilities but also because of better motivation. The report further states that the Negro and white children adjusted "constructively and in a friendly manner to the new situation."[23]

In one of the few available studies explicitly designed to test the influence of educational segregation upon personality characteristics, a standardized personality inventory and a measure of authoritarian versus democratic attitudes were administered to Negro freshmen and seniors enrolled in segregated and in integrated colleges.[24] The col-

[20] Stella Chess, K. B. Clark, and A. Thomas, "The Importance of Cultural Evaluation in Psychiatric Diagnosis and Treatment," *Psychiatric Quarterly*, 1953, 27, 102–114.

[21] Cf. F. Wertham, "Psychiatric Observations on Abolition of School Segregation," *Journal of Educational Sociology*, 1953, 26, 333–336.

[22] F. Wertham, *article cited*.

[23] F. Wertham, *article cited*, p. 335.

[24] H. M. Greenberg, "Some Effects of Segregated Education on Various Aspects of the Personality of Those Members of Disadvantaged Groups Experiencing This Form of Education," unpublished doctor's dissertation (New York University, 1955; microfilm).

leges were chosen so as to be closely equated in other variables, such as size, type of control, and socioeconomic level of students. It did not prove possible, however, to eliminate all differences besides segregation. Thus both integrated colleges were located in Midwestern states; but only one segregated college was in the Midwest, while the other was in a border state and followed for the most part a typical Southern pattern. Similarly, the majority of Negro students in the integrated colleges were of Midwestern origin, while those in the segregated colleges came chiefly from the South.

Mean scores showed that freshmen in the integrated colleges were significantly less neurotic and significantly more self-sufficient, self-confident, dominant, and democratic than those in segregated colleges. These differences may reflect in part selective factors in choice of colleges and in part the influence of previous educational and other environmental factors. In connection with the latter point, it was noted that the majority of freshmen in segregated colleges had also attended segregated elementary and high schools, while most of those in nonsegregated colleges had come from nonsegregated schools. Even more pertinent is the finding that mean score differences between segregated and integrated college students *increased* from the freshman to the senior years. Especially striking were the results obtained with the neuroticism scale, which showed significant improvement from freshman to senior year in integrated colleges but no significant change in segregated colleges. The one scale in which discrepant results were obtained was sociability. In this trait all differences were small and favored the segregated groups, although the only significant difference was that between segregated and unsegregated seniors. All other scales indicated better adjustment in integrated colleges, the differences increasing from freshman to senior years.

The far-reaching effects that racial segregation and discrimination may have upon personality are also evidenced by studies of adults through projective methods and clinical interviews. Projective techniques utilize relatively unstructured stimuli, such as inkblots or vague pictures, to induce the individual to "project" his own thoughts and feelings into the situation. Investigations with a number of these techniques have brought to light the characteristic anxieties, emotional conflicts, frustrations, aggression, and apathy resulting from the psychological milieu in which American Negroes generally live.[25] Further data on the emotional problems of American Negroes at different socioeconomic levels are provided by a series of detailed case reports of twenty-five Negro men and women, selected to represent lower, middle, and upper socioeconomic classes.[26] Each case was studied through psychoanalytic interviews, ranging in number from ten to over one hundred. Utilizing data obtained in these case studies, together with other information regarding Negro-white relations in America, the authors sought to demonstrate the effects of specific and identifiable cultural pressures on Negro personality. They concluded that the essential elements underlying the characteristic emotional difficulties of the American Negro are the low self-esteem and the aggressive tendencies induced by social discrimination. A wide range of behavior manifestations, from apathy and excessive submissiveness to overt antisocial acts, are described as different adaptations to these basic conditions.[27]

To be sure, all the observed effects of segregation upon personality development refer to segregation as currently practiced, with its associated discrimination, prejudice, and racial stereotypes. How far the same effects would occur as a result of a form of segregation that was stripped of these related conditions remains a purely academic question which is unanswerable within the framework of contemporary American culture. It is certainly doubtful whether enforced segregation can ever remain psychologically neutral. In any event, any sort of segregation that offers possible advantages, such as the educational segregation of mental defectives, gifted children, or students with different vocational objectives, is based upon relevant characteristics of the individual. As will be shown, however, it is the underlying fallacy of educational segregation by race that such segregation follows *irrelevant criteria.*

[25] Cf. B. P. Karon, *The Negro Personality* (New York: Springer, 1958); Georgene H. Seward, *Psychotherapy and Culture Conflict* (New York: Ronald Press, 1956), Ch. 6.

[26] A. Kardiner and L. Ovesey, *The Mark of Oppression: A Psychological Study of the American Negro* (New York: Norton, 1951).

[27] A. Kardiner and L. Ovesey, *op. cit.,* Ch. 9.

NEGRO-WHITE DIFFERENCES ON APTITUDE
AND ACHIEVEMENT TESTS

Comparisons of American Negroes and whites on intelligence tests have generally yielded significant mean differences in favor of whites. Such differences are significant in the statistical sense, which simply means that if the entire population from which the given samples are drawn were to be tested, a mean difference in favor of the same group would be expected. When the difference is said to be "significant at the 1 per cent level," the chances that the stated expectation is in error are one or less out of 100. This is the customary standard of certainty, or "significance level," set up for the acceptance of a hypothesis in scientific research. Mean Negro-white differences at the 1 per cent level of significance have been found in the testing of both adults and school-age children with both individual tests like the Binet and group tests of intelligence. The first large body of data on adult Negro-white differences in test performance was provided by the psychological examination of draftees during World War I. In this survey, the whites averaged significantly higher on both Army Alpha (a typical verbal intelligence test) and Army Beta (a nonlanguage test). Subsequent investigations of large groups of elementary, high school, and college students with both intelligence and educational achievement tests have yielded similar results.[28]

At the purely descriptive level, these findings are clear and consistent. The fundamental question that they leave unanswered, however, is that of causation. To what extent are the obtained differences in ability a result of the separate and *un*equal treatment received by whites and Negroes in educational facilities, vocational opportunities, and the more subtle psychological components of the cultural setting? To find that racial groups differ in behavior does not demonstrate that the differences are racial in origin. The latter would imply hereditary etiology traceable to genes that occur more frequently in one racial group than in another.

Many popular ideas about race are based upon a misunderstanding

[28] Leona E. Tyler, *The Psychology of Human Differences* (2nd ed.; New York: Appleton-Century-Crofts, 1956). Audrey M. Shuey, *The Testing of Negro Intelligence* (Lynchburg, Va.: Randolph-Macon Women's College, 1958); R. M. Dreger and K. S. Miller, "Comparative Psychological Studies of Negroes and Whites in the United States," *Psychological Bulletin*, 1960, 57, 361–402.

of the operation of heredity. It is beyond the scope of this discussion to explain the genetic mechanisms whereby racial differentiation in such physical traits as skin color and body build takes place. A particularly clear exposition of these processes can be found in Dobzhansky.[29] For the present purpose, it will suffice to note that, in the light of available genetic knowledge, it appears improbable that the racial differentiation which has taken place in physical traits was accompanied by differentiation with regard to genes affecting intellectual or personality development. It is *theoretically* more likely that behavioral differences between human populations result from cultural rather than from racial factors.[30]

If we examine the question of etiology from the viewpoint of *empirical* results, we find that the majority of investigations yield ambiguous data, owing to the presence of other variables besides race. A few approaches, however, permit a somewhat clearer analysis of contributing factors. For a more detailed consideration of both the results and the methodological and interpretative problems of race difference studies in general, the reader is referred to such sources as Anastasi,[31] Klineberg,[32] and Tyler.[33]

It is noteworthy that investigations at the *infant and preschool level* show that Negro-white differences are either highly reduced or completely nonexistent at these ages. In a study of 53 Negro infants in New Haven, for example, no significant inferiority to the white norms was found on the Gesell Developmental Schedules at a mean age of 26 weeks.[34] Follow-up of 40 cases at an average age of approximately

[29] T. Dobzhansky, "The Genetic Nature of Differences Among Men," in S. Persons (ed.), *Evolutionary Thought in America* (New Haven: Yale University Press, 1959), pp. 86–155; *Idem*, "Mendelian Populations and Their Evolution," in L. C. Dunn (ed.), *Genetics in the Twentieth Century* (New York: Macmillan, 1951), pp. 573–589.

[30] P. R. David and L. H. Snyder, "Genetic Variability and Human Behavior," in J. H. Rohrer and M. Sherif (eds.), *Social Psychology at the Crossroads* (New York: Harper & Brothers, 1951), pp. 53–82; T. Dobzhansky, "The Genetic Nature of Differences Among Men," *loc. cit.*

[31] Anne Anastasi, *Differential Psychology* (3rd ed.; New York: Macmillan, 1958), chaps. 16 and 17.

[32] O. Klineberg, *op. cit.*, Ch. 11.

[33] Leona E. Tyler, *op. cit.*, Ch. 11.

[34] Hilda Knobloch and B. Pasamanick, "Further Observations on the Behavioral Development of Negro Children," *Journal of Genetic Psychology*, 1953, 83, 137–157; B. Pasamanick, "A Comparative Study of the Behavior Development of Negro Infants," *Journal of Genetic Psychology*, 1946, 69, 3–44.

two years revealed no retardation. Mean quotients on different parts of the examination at this age ranged from 101 in language development to 125 in gross motor development. Normal performance on this scale is indicated by a quotient of 100. More detailed analysis of language performance revealed that the children were significantly better on items requiring verbal comprehension than on those calling for oral responsiveness in the course of the examination.[35] Among the factors to be considered in explanation of this finding are the influence of the white examiner, social pressures tending to inhibit verbalization in Negro children, and possibly a dawning awareness of racial stereotypes. In gross motor development, the Negro children were accelerated as compared with white children, and their performance was significantly better than in the language area. The investigators hypothesized that such acceleration results from the greater "permissiveness" of the lower-class homes in which the large majority of the Negro children were being reared, an explanation that was corroborated by a study of Negro children in Washington, D.C.[36]

Comparison of 113 Negro and 533 white infants in the Chicago area again showed no significant mean differences in either of two standardized infant intelligence scales.[37] In sharp contrast to these findings are the results of an earlier study of Negro and white infants in Florida.[38] In that study the whites excelled significantly on the Bühler Babytests, which cover a wide variety of functions but place somewhat more emphasis upon social behavior and problem-solving than is the case in most other infant scales. In explanation of these discrepant findings, other investigators[39] have pointed out that the white infants tested in the Florida study were also taller and heavier than the Negro infants. Such a difference in physical development

[35] Hilda Knobloch and B. Pasamanick, article cited; B. Pasamanick and Hilda Knobloch, "Early Language Behavior in Negro Children and the Testing of Intelligence," *Journal of Abnormal and Social Psychology*, 1955, 50, 401–402.

[36] Judith R. Williams and R. B. Scott, "Growth and Development of Negro Infants: IV. Motor Development and Its Relationship to Child Rearing Practices in Two Groups of Negro Infants," *Child Development*, 1953, 24, 103–121.

[37] A. R. Gilliland, "Socioeconomic Status and Race as Factors in Infant Intelligence Test Scores," *Child Development*, 1951, 22, 271–273.

[38] Myrtle B. McGraw, "A Comparative Study of a Group of Southern White and Negro Infants," *Genetic Psychology Monographs*, 1931, 10, 1–105.

[39] Hilda Knobloch and B. Pasamanick, "Further Observations on the Behavioral Development of Negro Children," article cited; B. Pasamanick, article cited.

may have resulted from inequalities in prenatal and postnatal care and nutrition. Differences in maternal diet are particularly important in this connection. In the New Haven group, the heights and weights of the Negro infants exceeded those found in the Florida group and approached the white norms. Owing to economic and social reasons, the diet of Florida Negroes in the late 1920's was undoubtedly inferior to that of New Haven Negroes in the early 1940's. Such a nutritional difference may account for both the physical and behavioral retardation of the former group.[40]

Tests of Negro preschool children have likewise revealed no significant inferiority as compared to white norms. A group of 91 Negro kindergarten children in Minneapolis were found to have a mean Stanford-Binet IQ of 100.78.[41] The investigator pointed out, however, that by the sixth and seventh grade, Negro children in Minneapolis public schools usually declined to the IQ level reported in other studies. It might be added that a group of 341 white kindergarten children tested in the same study obtained a mean Stanford-Binet IQ of 107.06, which was significantly higher than that of the Negro children. However, the two groups differed extensively in the occupational level of the fathers. The whites represented a random sample of the general population in this respect, while the Negroes came largely from the skilled and unskilled labor classes. When Negro children were compared with white children in the corresponding occupational levels, no significant difference in mean IQ remained.

In a study conducted in New York City, measures of language development and IQ on a nonverbal test (Goodenough Draw-a-Man Test) were obtained on 100 five-year-old Negro and white children attending Department of Welfare day care centers.[42] The subjects included 25 Negroes and 25 whites living in segregated neighborhoods and 25 Negroes and 25 whites living in interracial neighborhoods. Sex ratio was approximately the same in each subgroup. Socioeconomic and other background factors were relatively uniform in all

[40] Ruth F. Harrell, Ella Woodyard, and A. I. Gates, *The Effect of Mothers' Diets on the Intelligence of the Offspring* (New York: Bureau of Publications, Teachers College, Columbia University, 1955).

[41] F. Brown, article cited.

[42] Anne Anastasi and Rita Y. D'Angelo, "A Comparison of Negro and White Preschool Children in Language Development and Goodenough Draw-a-Man IQ," *Journal of Genetic Psychology*, 1952, 81, 147–165.

groups. No significant race difference was found in the Draw-a-Man IQ. Analysis of spontaneous speech samples, in terms of both sentence length and maturity of sentence structure, revealed a number of significant differences favoring whites in segregated neighborhoods, but only one significant difference in the same direction in interracial neighborhoods. In the interpretation of relative findings with the Draw-a-Man test and the spontaneous speech samples, it should again be borne in mind that all measures were obtained by a white examiner.

As a result of recent research on the nature of intelligence and the organization of psychological traits, there has been an increasing tendency to investigate group differences in separate abilities rather than in composite, global measures such as the IQ. Studies on the American Negro have shown more inferiority on *perceptual and spatial functions* than on most types of verbal tasks. Negro children score particularly low on tests requiring the visualization of spatial relations and the mental rearrangement of geometric figures.[43] When Negro and white boys were matched on total Stanford-Binet IQ and their performance on individual items was compared, the Negroes excelled on the rearrangement of disarranged sentences, memory for sentences, and vocabulary, while the whites surpassed them on arithmetic reasoning, repeating digits backwards, and detecting absurdities in pictures.[44] Similar results have been found with other intelligence tests, and with both adults and children.[45] It should also be noted that differences in the same direction are obtained in comparisons between Northern and Southern Negroes, the Northern Negroes

[43] K. L. Bean, "Negro Responses to Verbal and Non-Verbal Test Material," *Journal of Psychology*, 1942, 13, 343–353; T. E. Neyland and W. C. Lawrence, "Chicago Non-Verbal Examination Results on an East Tennessee Negro Population," *Journal of Clinical Psychology*, 1953, 9, 44–46.

[44] D. P. Clarke, "Stanford-Binet Scale L Response Patterns in Matched Racial Groups," *Journal of Negro Education*, 1941, 10, 230–238.

[45] K. S. Davidson, *et al.*, "A Preliminary Study of Negro and White Differences on Form I of the Wechsler-Bellevue Scale," *Journal of Consulting Psychology*, 1950, 14, 489–492; W. P. De Stephens, "Are Criminals Morons?", *Journal of Social Psychology*, 1953, 38, 187–199; J. C. Franklin, "Discriminative Value and Patterns of the Wechsler-Bellevue Scales in the Examination of Delinquent Negro Boys," *Educational and Psychological Measurement*, 1945, 5, 71–85; E. F. Hammer, "Comparison of the Performance of Negro Children and Adolescents on Two Tests of Intelligence, One an Emergency Scale," *Journal of Genetic Psychology*, 1954, 84, 85–93.

tending to excel the Southern more on spatial-perceptual than on verbal tests.[46]

A number of factors in the cultural background of the American Negro may help to explain such findings. Performance tests usually put a higher premium on speed than do verbal tests. And the typical environment of the American Negro—especially in the South—provides little inducement for developing habits of rapid work. A second contributing factor may be found in the culturally determined Negro attitude of passive compliance as contrasted to active exploration. Such an attitude is more conducive to rote verbal learning than to perceptual manipulation of stimuli and problem-solving.

Also relevant is Hebb's hypothesis that early perceptual learning influences subsequent intellectual development.[47] As originally formulated, this hypothesis referred, not to group differences in test performance, but to fundamental learning theory. Corroborative data have been obtained in controlled experiments on the effects of early experiences upon subsequent problem-solving ability of rats,[48] dogs,[49] and primates.[50] The findings of these studies raise considerable doubt regarding the traditional view that learning ability is genetically determined and relatively unmodifiable. With regard to the test performance of Negro children, it is possible that impoverishment of early perceptual experience in the underprivileged environment of the lower-class Negro home and segregated school may have retarded the development of certain intellectual functions, especially those pertaining to spatial aptitudes and problem-solving.

Some corroboration of the hypothesis of early perceptual handicap is to be found in studies of the relative effects of perceptual training on Negro and white performance. In one investigation, Negro and white high school students received training in the visual discrimina-

[46] S. Machover, "Cultural and Racial Variations in Patterns of Intellect," Teachers College *Contributions to Education,* 1943, No. 875.

[47] D. O. Hebb, *The Organization of Behavior* (New York: Wiley, 1949).

[48] Cf. F. A. Beach and J. Jaynes, "Effects of Early Experience upon the Behavior of Animals," *Psychological Bulletin,* 1954, 51, 255–256.

[49] W. R. Thompson and W. Heron, "The Effects of Restricting Early Experience on the Problem-Solving Capacity of Dogs," *Canadian Journal of Psychology,* 1954, 8, 17–31.

[50] H. F. Harlow, "The Formation of Learning Sets," *Psychological Review,* 1949, 56, 51–65 .

tion of length.[51] Although the whites excelled initially, the Negroes benefited more from training and the difference between the two groups diminished with training. Even more relevant is an experiment with Negro and white primary school children.[52] Group intelligence tests were administered in January and in May. During the intervening period, one-half of the Negro and one-half of the white children received practice with problems involving visual perception, discrimination, and spatial relations. The intelligence tests showed significant increases following such training, the Negro children improving more than the white and retaining their gains on a later retest in October. Moreover, Negro gains were greater on the nonlanguage than on the language tests.

Reference should likewise be made to so-called *culture-free tests*.[53] Such tests are specially designed for use in comparative studies of persons reared in different cultures or subcultures. It should be noted, however, that no test can be truly culture-free. Since a psychological test is only a standardized measure of a behavior sample, any condition that influences behavior will be reflected in test scores. Nevertheless, it is theoretically possible to construct a test that presupposes only experience common to different cultures. Although not *free* from cultural influences, such a test would utilize only elements *common* to all cultures. This is what available "culture-free" tests have undertaken to do.

In actual practice, however, such tests fall short of their objective in many respects. No existing test is entirely unrestricted in its cultural reference. The difference between "culture-free" and other tests is one of degree. The mere use of paper and pencil or the presentation of abstract tasks that have no immediate practical significance will favor some cultural groups and handicap others. Other relevant factors that differ among cultures or subcultures include intrinsic interest of test content, extent of familiarity with pictorial or diagrammatic representation, rapport with the examiner (especially if he belongs to

[51] O. W. Eagleson, "Comparative Studies of White and Negro Subjects in Learning to Discriminate Visual Magnitude," *Journal of Psychology*, 1937, 4, 167–197.

[52] J. H. Boger, "An Experimental Study of the Effects of Perceptual Training on Group IQ Test Scores," *Journal of Educational Research*, 1952, 46, 43–52.

[53] Cf. Anne Anastasi, *Psychological Testing* (2nd ed.; New York: Macmillan, 1961), pp. 255–268.

a different race from that of the testees), drive to perform well on a test, competitive desire to excel others, and previously developed problem-solving attitudes.

The sort of misinterpretation that may arise when test content is categorically described as "culture-free" or "noncultural" is illustrated by a study conducted with Negro and white high school seniors in Pennsylvania and New Jersey.[54] All subjects were given two sets of test questions, equated in difficulty but differing in cultural content as determined by judges' ratings. Each judge was left free to define "cultural" as he chose. A comparison of the questions classified in the "cultural" and in the "noncultural" sets indicates that "cultural" was closely identified with verbal content and with dependence upon schooling. Yet these are not the principal ways in which the cultural backgrounds of the Negro and white subjects employed in this particular investigation differed. Since all were high school students enrolled in the same classes, schooling was presumably more uniform than home background. Moreover, the American Negro is not bilingual, and hence his linguistic deficiency should be no greater than that in other intellectual functions, especially when no oral responses are required. The so-called noncultural questions, on the other hand, made relatively heavy demands on perceptual and spatial aptitudes, in which other studies have shown the Negro to be relatively deficient. In view of these characteristics of the items, it is not surprising to find that the Negro students in this study scored significantly poorer on the "noncultural" than on the "cultural" items.

GROUP DIFFERENCES AND THE INDIVIDUAL

When Samuel Johnson was asked which is more intelligent, man or woman, he is reported to have replied, "Which man, which woman?" This remark highlights an important fact about all group comparisons, namely, that wide individual differences exist within each group, with a consequent *overlapping* between groups. Even when one group excels another by a large and significant amount, individuals can be

[54] F. C. J. McGurk, "Comparison of the Performance of Negro and White High School Seniors on Cultural and Noncultural Psychological Test Questions," unpublished doctor's dissertation (Catholic University, 1951; microcard); *Idem*, "On White and Negro Test Performance and Socioeconomic Factors," *Journal of Abnormal and Social Psychology*, 1953, 48, 448–450.

found in the "inferior" group who surpass individuals in the "superior" group. Owing to the large extent of individual differences within any one group, as contrasted to the relatively small differences between group averages, an individual's group membership is a very unreliable basis for predicting his standing in most psychological traits.

Group comparisons are generally reported in terms of means or other group characteristics. For a more complete picture, such information is often supplemented by some measure of overlapping, such as the percentage of persons in one group who reach or exceed the mean (or median) of the other group. It is well to have clearly in mind just what such "percentage of overlap" actually means. In Figure 1 will be found two schematic distributions illustrating what is often loosely described as "30 per cent overlap." More precisely, this statement signifies that 30 per cent of one group reach or exceed the median of the other, as indicated by the shaded area. Such a degree of overlap is close to that usually found between psychological test scores of Negroes and whites in the United States. In the interpretation of percentage overlap, it should be noted that, when the two distributions coincide and overlapping is complete, 50 per cent of one group reach or exceed the median of the other. This follows from the fact that, within any single distribution, 50 per cent of the cases fall at or above the group median. The reported percentage overlap must thus be evaluated in terms of 50, rather than 100, as the possible upper limit.

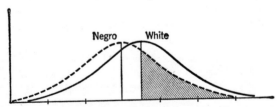

Fig. 1. Schematic Distributions Illustrating "30 Per Cent Overlap"*

One implication of the degree of overlap shown in Figure 1 is that, if a Negro were to be chosen at random from his group, the chances

* Reproduced by permission from *Differential Psychology*, by Anne Anastasi, (3rd ed. New York: The Macmillan Company, 1958), p. 549, © The Macmillan Company 1958.

are 30 out of 100 that his score would reach or exceed that of the *average white*. Thus if we were to assume that a Negro is inferior to the white median, under these conditions, we would be in error 30 out of 100 times. Such an error ratio may be compared to the "1 per cent level of significance" customarily required before accepting a conclusion as established in scientific research. In that case, the chances of being in error are only one out of 100. It is thus apparent that, owing to the extensive overlapping of test scores, a knowledge of the individual's group membership does not permit us to predict his relative test performance with an acceptable degree of certainty.

Another noteworthy point concerns the total amount of overlapping of the distributions. If 30 per cent of the Negroes reach or exceed the white median, the percentage of Negroes who reach or exceed the lowest score of the white group will be approximately 99. Under these conditions, therefore, the ranges will overlap almost completely. It would thus be likely that the best performers in both groups would obtain scores that are about equally high, and the poorest in both groups would score about equally low.

Other implications of overlapping can be seen by reference to certain empirical findings regarding Negro test performance. For example, *regional differences* among Negroes, as well as among whites, are so large as to reverse completely the relative standing of the two races when extreme subgroups are compared. A classic illustration is provided by the state-by-state analysis of Army Alpha scores during World War I. The results showed that the median Alpha scores of Negroes from Illinois, New York, Ohio, and Pennsylvania were *higher* than the median Alpha scores of whites from Arkansas, Georgia, Kentucky, and Mississippi.[55] These data furnish a vivid demonstration of the extensive overlapping between the total white and Negro populations. Not only could many individuals be found in the Negro distribution who excelled individuals in the white distribution, but also local groups could be found in the Negro population that surpassed other local groups in the white population.

Studies of *intellectually gifted Negro children* may be regarded as a further illustration of the range of individual differences found within the Negro population and the overlapping between Negro and

---

[55] R. M. Yerkes (ed.), "Psychological Examining in the United States Army," *Memoirs of the National Academy of Sciences*, 1921, 15.

white distributions. Witty and his students[56] have published a number of test surveys, case studies, and follow-ups of Negro children whose IQ's ranged from 120 to 200. Like white children of corresponding IQ, these intellectually superior Negro children tended to excel in height, weight, and general physical development; they were on the whole superior in character and personality; and their parents had more than average education and tended to cluster in the higher occupational levels.

Of particular interest is the analysis of proportion of white admixture among gifted Negro children. In one of the studies cited above, 63 Negro children with IQ's of 125 or higher were classified into four categories of race mixture on the basis of genealogical data obtained from the parents.[57] The results revealed no consistent tendency for the proportion of white ancestry to be larger in the gifted groups than in the general Negro population. It is also interesting to note that the highest IQ in the group, 200, was obtained by a Negro girl whose ancestry showed no evidence of white mixture.[58] It may be added parenthetically that general surveys of Negro school children and college students have likewise yielded no evidence of significant correlation between proportion of white ancestry and intelligence test performance.[59] Such findings are consistent with an environmental interpretation of Negro-white differences in test scores,

---

[56] M. D. Jenkins, "A Socio-Psychological Study of Negro Children of Superior Intelligence," unpublished doctor's dissertation (Northwestern University, 1935); *Idem*, "Case Studies of Negro Children of Binet IQ 160 and Above," *Journal of Negro Education*, 1943, 12, 159–166; *Idem*, "The Upper Limit of Ability Among American Negroes," *Scientific Monthly*, 1948, 46, 399–401; V. Theman and P. Witty, "Case Studies and Genetic Records of Two Gifted Negroes," *Journal of Psychology*, 1943, 15, 165–181; P. A. Witty and M. D. Jenkins, "Intra-Race Testing and Negro Intelligence," *Journal of Psychology*, 1936, 1, 179–192; P. Witty and V. Theman, "A Follow-Up Study of the Educational Attainment of Gifted Negroes," *Journal of Educational Psychology*, 1943, 34, 35–47.

[57] P. A. Witty and M. D. Jenkins, "Intra-Race Testing and Negro Intelligence," article cited.

[58] V. Theman and P. Witty, *article cited*; P. A. Witty and M. D. Jenkins, *article cited*.

[59] M. J. Herskovits, "On the Relation Between Negro-White Mixture and Standing in Intelligence Tests," *Journal of Genetic Psychology*, 1926, 33, 30–42; O. Klineberg, "An Experimental Study of Speed and Other Factors in 'Racial' Differences," *Archives of Psychology*, 1928, No. 93; J. Peterson and L. H. Lanier, "Studies in the Comparative Abilities of Whites and Negroes," *Mental Measurement Monographs*, 1929, No. 5.

since in the contemporary American culture individuals with any known or discernible Negro ancestry are classified and treated as Negroes.

In the light of the extensive overlapping of distributions, it is abundantly clear that differences between group means, even when statistically significant, may be of little practical value for dealing with individuals. Mean differences *between* groups are always far smaller than differences *within* groups. There is no short cut to the understanding of people, no possibility of learning the peculiarities of a few broad groups into which individuals can then be conveniently pigeonholed. In human relations, the only proper unit is the individual.

The implications of overlapping for the question of educational desegregation are obvious. Any educational selection or classification on the basis of race would inevitably lead to unwarranted discrimination against individuals and to waste of human resources. This would be true regardless of the causes of existing mean differences in abilities between Negroes and whites. But the scientist is not satisfied with a description of the *status quo*. He wants to trace observed events to their sources. Only thus will he be able to predict how his descriptive findings may be modified as conditions change. The problems to be considered in the next two sections bear directly on the causation of observed Negro-white differences in psychological traits.

EFFECTS OF EDUCATION UPON TESTED INTELLIGENCE

That intelligence test scores are affected by the amount and nature of schooling the individual has received is now generally recognized by psychologists. Evidence in support of this conclusion may be found in longitudinal studies of the same individuals, as well as in cross-sectional studies of comparable populations tested over long intervals of time.[60] Among the former are two investigations in which boys who had been tested upon completion of uniform elementary schooling were reexamined after ten years in one study and after twenty years in the other.[61] Both investigators found significant re-

[60] Cf. Anne Anastasi, *Differential Psychology, op. cit.,* chap. 7.
[61] T. Husén, "The Influence of Schooling upon IQ," *Theoria,* 1951, 17, 61–88; I. Lorge, "Schooling Makes a Difference," *Teachers College Record,* 1945, 46, 483–492.

lationships between the amount of subsequent education and retest performance, when the effect of initial scores was ruled out. Similarly, college freshmen retested after a lapse of thirty years showed mean gains in test scores which increased consistently with amount of college or graduate training received after the initial test.[62]

Cross-sectional surveys of community-wide or nation-wide samples have likewise revealed significant rises in mean test scores as socio-economic and educational facilities improved. This is illustrated by the Scottish surveys of nearly complete samples of eleven-year-old children tested in 1932 and 1947,[63] by a study of American high school students over a twenty-year period,[64] by a comparison of the intelligence test performance of American soldiers during the two world wars,[65] and by ten-year retests in a rural Tennessee community that had made rapid progress in social and educational conditions during the interval.[66]

Turning to studies concerned directly with the American Negro, we find the most relevant data in research on regional differences. First it should be noted that Northern Negroes have consistently excelled Southern Negroes in mean test scores. This difference has been demonstrated with varied samples, including draftees in both world wars, college students, and school children.[67] Moreover, the regional difference persists when comparisons are made between groups matched in occupational level.

Two contrasting hypotheses could account for these differences between Northern and Southern Negroes. According to one hypothesis, the superiority of Northern Negroes results from *selective migration*, the more intelligent and ambitious individuals tending to migrate to more favorable areas. The other hypothesis explains the regional differences in ability on the basis of dissimilar educational

[62] W. A. Owens, Jr., "Age and Mental Abilities: A Longitudinal Study," *Genetic Psychology Monographs*, 1953, 48, 3–54.

[63] Scottish Council for Research in Education, *The Trend of Scottish Intelligence* (London: University of London Press, 1949).

[64] F. H. Finch, "Enrollment Increases and Changes in the Mental Level of the High School Population," *Applied Psychology Monographs*, 1946, No. 10.

[65] R. D. Tuddenham, "Soldier Intelligence in World Wars I and II," *American Psychologist*, 1948, 3, 54–56.

[66] L. R. Wheeler, "A Comparative Study of the Intelligence of East Tennessee Mountain Children," *Journal of Educational Psychology*, 1942, 33, 321–334.

[67] Cf. Anne Anastasi, *Differential Psychology, op. cit.*, chap. 17.

and other *environmental facilities* under which Negro children are reared in the North and the South. The environmental differences would include not only absolute inequalities in socioeconomic and educational conditions that characterize these regions as a whole, but also discrepancies in the relative position of Negroes and whites in the North and the South.

The first hypothesis implies that the migrating individuals were superior from the outset, the second that they improved after migration. Tests of these two hypotheses have been conducted by checking the school performance of migrating children prior to migration, and by comparing groups that had attended Northern schools for varying periods.[68] A more recent study of Negro children in Philadelphia utilized a longitudinal approach and thus provides more conclusive data.[69] In this study, initial and retest IQ's of Negro children with varying periods of Northern residence were analyzed. The Southern-born Negro children in the total sample were classified with reference to grade level at which they entered Philadelphia schools, ranging from 1A to 9A. In addition, test scores were obtained from a control group of Philadelphia-born Negro children in the same schools. Among the latter, it is interesting to note that a subgroup that had attended kindergarten scored higher than the subgroup with no kindergarten experience. This difference appeared on the 1A tests and remained on subsequent retests. The advantage of the kindergarten group may result from selective factors in kindergarten enrollment, or from the effect of early perceptual and other relevant training in kindergarten, or from a combination of both types of causes.

Within each of the Philadelphia-born groups, however, there is no consistent tendency for scores to rise upon retesting, the successive means exhibiting only chance fluctuations. This finding contrasts sharply with the results obtained with Southern-born Negro children who had migrated to Philadelphia. In each of the latter groups, there

[68] O. Klineberg, *Negro Intelligence and Selective Migration* (New York: Columbia University Press, 1935); H. H. Long, "The Intelligence of Colored Elementary Pupils in Washington, D.C.," *Journal of Negro Education,* 1934, 3, 205–222.

[69] E. S. Lee, "Negro Intelligence and Selective Migration: A Philadelphia Test of the Klineberg Hypothesis," *American Sociological Review,* 1951, 16, 227–233.

is a significant tendency for mean scores to improve with increasing length of Northern residence. Thus the mean IQ of the group entering Philadelphia schools in 1A rises from 86.5 upon school entrance to 92.8 in grade 9A; the group transferring to Philadelphia schools in 1B or 2B rises from 86.7 to 90.5, and so on for the other Southern-born groups. It is also noteworthy that the earlier the children had entered a Northern school, the higher their IQ in any one grade. Corroborative data for all the above findings were obtained with tests of separate aptitudes which were also administered to some or all subjects in this study. With one minor exception, all tests showed rising mean scores with increasing length of Northern residence, as well as significant superiority of the group that had attended kindergarten. Thus the results of this study, together with those of earlier similar investigations, support the hypothesis that differences in test scores between Northern and Southern Negroes result from environmental inequalities rather than from selective migration.

The Concept of Environment

We sometimes hear the claim that Negro children do more poorly than white children on intelligence tests, even when they have the same environment. But are their environments ever the *same?* In most comparisons of the test performance of Negroes and whites, no attempt has been made to keep environment constant; the data are merely descriptive of the behavior of the two groups under existing environmental inequalities. A few investigators, however, have made special efforts to obtain groups of whites and Negroes that were equated in environmental variables. It is therefore appropriate to examine these studies more closely, with special reference to methodology.

In a study conducted in Canada, the subjects were Negro and white children attending the same schools.[70] Educational facilities were thus controlled. Nevertheless, the Negro and white children differed significantly in the socioeconomic levels of their homes. Moreover, it was found that the white children attended school more regularly than the Negro, a difference which is often associated with social

[70] H. A. Tanser, *The Settlement of Negroes in Kent County, Ontario* (Chatham, Ont.: Author, 1939).

class differences. Thus within the entire sample of white children tested, school attendance averaged 93.38 per cent; within the Negro sample, it averaged 84.77 per cent.

Another investigator tested Negro and white children in a poor rural district in Virginia, endeavoring to control both educational and socioeconomic variables.[71] Education, however, was equated only by choosing segregated Negro and white schools with the same teacher-pupil ratio, other differences between the schools remaining uncontrolled. In the same study, subgroups of 49 Negro and 49 white children were matched on a socioeconomic scale based on various characteristics of the home and parents. Negro-white differences in intelligence test scores were reduced but not eliminated in these matched subgroups. The investigator noted, moreover, that the scale employed is not well suited to the groups studied, since it does not discriminate adequately at very low socioeconomic levels, where most of the subjects fell. In addition, a number of items on this scale may not have the same meaning when applied to Negro and white homes.

A more recent study was likewise designed to control both educational and socioeconomic factors.[72] The subjects were Negro and white high school seniors in Pennsylvania and New Jersey. The 213 Negro and 213 white subjects chosen for study were attending the same schools and were enrolled in the same curricula. In addition, Negroes and whites were matched on eleven socioeconomic items. Again it appears unlikely that the items used can be entirely comparable when applied to Negroes and whites. Among such items, for example, is the father's occupational level, classified into two categories: professional, business, and clerical versus skilled and unskilled labor. It is highly probable that relatively more Negroes than whites fell near the bottom of each of these broad occupational categories. Even if specific occupations had been matched, it could not be assumed that socioeconomic level had been equated. The home of an average Negro doctor and an average white doctor, for example, would be likely to differ widely in income level and in many other characteristics. Another important uncontrolled factor in this, as in

[71] Myrtle Bruce, "Factors Affecting Intelligence Test Performance of Whites and Negroes," *Archives of Psychology,* 1940, No. 252.
[72] F. C. J. McGurk, "Comparison of the Performance of Negro and White High School Seniors," etc., *op. cit.; Idem,* "On White and Negro Test Performance," etc., article cited.

other studies cited, is that of social stereotypes and related motivational differences.

In the present connection, some clarification of the concept of environment itself may be appropriate. To the psychologist, environment connotes much more than it does in popular usage. In psychological terms, environment may be defined as the sum total of the stimuli to which the individual responds from conception until death. Certain aspects of this definition merit special emphasis.

Environment covers a vast multiplicity of variables. Under the comprehensive term, "environment," are included characteristics of the community, the neighborhood, the school, and the home. The individual variables may be as broad as income level or as narrow as a particular TV program that the family habitually tunes in after dinner. Qualitatively they may range from food and medical care to chemistry sets and comic books. An important part of the developing child's environment consists of the people with whom he interacts—children as well as adults. Recent psychological research has focused attention especially upon child-rearing practices—their characteristic differences among socioeconomic and ethnic groups and their influence upon emotional and intellectual development. All these factors and many more are a part of the child's environment.

Environment includes psychological as well as physical conditions. Environment comprises the social, emotional, and spiritual climate of home, church, classroom, and playground. It includes the beliefs, preferences, and attitudes of one's associates. An important psychological element in the individual's environment is social expectancy. This factor operates to perpetuate group stereotypes with regard to race, nationality, sex, physical type, and other characteristics. What is expected of an individual tends to influence what he does. When such expectation has the force of cultural tradition behind it and is repeatedly corroborated in nearly all contacts with associates, it is difficult not to succumb to it. As a result, the individual often becomes convinced that he is intellectually inferior or superior, or that he possesses this or that talent or defect according to the dictates of his particular culture. From an early age, the minority group child becomes aware of the characteristic behavior traits associated with his racial or national stereotype. In his daily contacts with family, playmates, teachers, and other adults, he finds constant reminders of what is expected of him. Gradually these expectations become part of his own self-concept, which in turn affects his motivation and achievement. By these means, social expectancy tends to determine what a person becomes.

Environment begins to operate before birth. It is now well established that numerous factors in the prenatal environment may exert a pronounced influence upon behavioral as well as structural properties of the organism. Both animal experiments and clinical observations of human cases have demonstrated the part played by prenatal physical and chemical conditions in the development of bodily anomalies and of many well known varieties of mental deficiency.[73] Of special interest is the finding that inadequacies of maternal diet may have a retarding effect upon the child's intellectual development. In a well controlled experiment,[74] children whose mothers had received a dietary supplement during pregnancy and lactation obtained significantly higher mean IQ's when tested at the ages of three and four years than did children whose mothers had received a control pill. The mothers who served as subjects in this experiment were all in low-income groups and the majority were Negroes.

Another illustration of the far-reaching effects that prenatal environmental deficiencies may have upon behavior development is provided by a series of studies on large samples of Negroes and whites in Baltimore.[75] This research showed that complications of pregnancy and parturition are significantly related to mental defect and behavior disorders in the offspring. An important source of such irregularities in the process of childbearing and birth is to be found in poor maternal nutrition and other conditions associated with low socioeconomic status. Analysis of the data revealed a higher frequency of all such medical complications in lower than in higher socioeconomic levels, and a higher frequency among Negroes than among whites. Here, then, is an example of cultural differentials producing

[73] Cf. Anne Anastasi, *Differential Psychology, op. cit.,* chap. 3, 12; S. B. Sarason, *Psychological Problems in Mental Deficiency* (3rd. ed.; New York: Harper & Brothers, 1939).

[74] Ruth F. Harrell, Ella Woodyard, and A. I. Gates, *op. cit.*

[75] B. Pasamanick, Hilda Knobloch, and A. M. Lilienfeld, "Socioeconomic Status and Some Precursors of Neuropsychiatric Disorders," *American Journal of Orthopsychiatry,* 1956, 26, 594–601.

structural or physiological deficiencies, which in turn lead to behavioral inadequacies or disorders.

Environmental factors, whatever their nature, may produce permanent and irreversible effects upon the developing individual. Many of the deleterious conditions leading to brain injury prior to, during, or after birth would fall into this category. Similarly, adverse experiential factors operating over many years may cause intellectual or emotional damage that can no longer be corrected at the time when remedial measures are instituted. To be sure, many behavioral deficiencies *are* remediable—through medical treatment, psychotherapy, counseling, and special training programs. Others cannot be remedied within the individual's lifetime, but require more than one generation for their abolition. It must be emphasized, however, that neither the permanence nor the organic basis of a psychological deficiency implies hereditary origin. Nor does the existence of such deficiencies justify a failure to rectify the very environmental conditions that induced them.

SUMMARY

Psychological research provides data bearing on educational desegregation from a number of angles. Social psychologists have investigated the conditions under which the individual acquires racial attitudes in the process of growing up in a particular cultural milieu. They have also demonstrated that such attitudes are modifiable; and they have studied the relation of various individual characteristics and situational factors to attitude changes. Clinical observations and personality research have thrown light upon the effects of racial segregation on personality development. For the minority group member, segregation tends to produce low self-esteem and feelings of inferiority and frustration. Either apathy or aggression may be the overt expression of such feelings. The low achievement motivation that usually results may in turn retard the individual's educational progress and intellectual development.

On intelligence tests, the average performance of Negroes has generally been lower than that of whites. Although statistically significant, such group differences must be qualified in two important respects. First, they represent only a description of differences under existing cultural conditions, but provide no evidence for the racial or hereditary origin of such differences. Although controlled investigations are difficult to conduct in this area, what little evidence is available on the causes of group differences points more strongly toward a cultural than a biological interpretation. A second necessary qualification stems from the wide individual differences within groups and the consequent overlapping of groups. As a result, group averages provide a very unreliable guide to the evaluation of individuals.

Of special relevance to the problems of educational segregation and desegregation are data on the effects of education itself upon intelligence test performance. Both amount and quality of education are reflected in the individual's test score. Among Negro groups, studies on regional differences and on the effects of migration also point up the influence of education and other community variables upon a child's IQ.

Negro and white groups allegedly equated in environment are not truly comparable in all important environmental factors. Environment comprises not only such familiar elements as schooling facilities and socioeconomic level of the home, but also a vast array of other conditions, from prenatal nutrition to social stereotypes. The psychological effects of environment range over a wide continuum, from the transitory and superficial, through more lasting but still modifiable characteristics, to some that cannot be altered within a single lifetime.

A Positive Approach to the Social Question

JOHN LA FARGE

If, as a complete stranger, I were to record an overmastering impression from the six preceding essays in this volume, I might say: they conclusively analyze and destroy the image of the current American Negro as a congenitally inferior person. On a walk around the town I can of course run into a boundless variety of Negro individuals: good, bad, and indifferent. But one point these essays have clearly established. Where the less favored of the city's multitudes have fallen short of the mark of excellence—and there are plenty of such instances—they are not "that way" because of their inherited genes, but by reason of the many retarding factors that can produce degradation in any variety of human beings: no more than this, no less.

From this reading one learns more than this merely negative conclusion. The essays emphasize the status of the Negro as a citizen of our republic, involved in our country's history at every step. They sketch his natural dignity as a human being, and open our eyes to the supernatural dignity that he enjoys as a member of the Church, of the Mystical Body of Jesus Christ. They show, in short, that when we speak of Negroes in this country we are not talking about mere census figures, but are discussing people, in the fullest sense of the word.

For some readers, such a readjustment of views can be most disturbing. It means the shattering of concepts about one's fellow human being to which we have tenaciously clung from our earliest years. It can mean, in other words, a new image of the Negro. If I pursue the matter, I find this means not only that the white man, from the sheer weight of facts, is obliged to form a concept of his Negro fellow citizen very different from that which he has always more or less naturally accepted. It means likewise that the Negro has learned to form a very different image of himself: that he—or she—particularly the Negro youth—is prepared to act upon that image, and cut through a jumbled mass of accepted misapprehensions by striking out in new and heretofore unused paths.

It is not enough, however, merely to destroy a false conception. We are dealing not with Stoic philosophers, but with living, passionate human beings. The dead weight of long generations of degradation and misunderstanding cannot be overcome by mere enlightenment as to the error of our ways: useful and all-necessary as this clarification may be. A problem has been posed—what is the real situation, in the widest sense, of the American Negro? That question has been answered: it is the situation, tragic and painful, of a human being like ourselves. A problem has been proposed, as well as the answer to it. But an ingredient is yet to be supplied, and that is the positive note of hope. An instance may make this clear.

I

In the autumn of 1960 the nation at large was pretty well stirred up over the determination shown by two young Atlanta Negroes, Charlayne Hunter and Hamilton Holmes, to enter as freshmen at the University of Georgia, an all-white institution, where no Negro had ever before been matriculated. After a sharp initial setback they suc-

ceeded in vindicating their rights, and managed to enroll peacefully
in the university. In so doing they made cordial friends among students and faculty alike. In discussing the experience with Miss Hunter
a few months later on the occasion of her visit to New York City to
receive a testimonial, what I found uppermost in her mind was the
note of hope—hope grounded in the cordial attitude of so many of
her fellow students, hope that by their own personal triumph over
the forces of fear and prejudice they would be able to bring new
meaning to the life of the university itself. Moreover, her own spirit
of confidence reflected the persistently hopeful note of her own pastor
in Atlanta, Father Anthony Walsh, C.P.

The same spirit of hope had started Mrs. Rosa Parks walking from
her home to her work when she was denied proper seating accommodations on the bus in Montgomery, Alabama, and started thousands of other Negro men and women walking in the same city under
the leadership of Dr. Martin Luther King. Such hope gave courage
to young Joseph McNeill and his three student companions to start the
sit-in movement in the segregated public-service restaurants in the
South, and led Mrs. Gabrielle, a white mother of children in New
Orleans to defy inhuman blasts of hatred and abuse and quietly send
her children to an integrated public school.

Instances would be easy enough to multiply. They are part of the
epic of our modern times. But the meaning of this epic is apt to elude
us unless we look a bit more sharply at the facts.

Today, it is no longer possible for the intelligent and progressive
Negro to drift complacently with the times, to hope that something
will somehow turn up and make life pleasant and relatively successful. In simpler days, he could somehow accommodate himself to a
second-class citizenship. There were service jobs fairly handy, where
he could manage to make out. As for his children, they would somehow accommodate themselves and he would hope for the best.

But for an ever-increasing circle of Negroes such patriarchal days
are definitely past. Modern industrial civilization with its correlative
in modern industrial organization raises spiky barriers. It's all very
well for a Negro youth and future father of a family to wangle a fair
mechanical education out of a Northern industrial high school. But
what does such a training mean when, for instance, out of 6,000 ap-
prenticeships in a given industry only four are open to Negroes?

A survey by the Associated Press, released on April 23, 1961, revealed in the Southern states an almost total lack—except for jobs involving Federal contracts—of laws on which to base comprehensive litigation in the employment field. There was also fear that if job opportunities were fully equal, there would not be enough qualified Negroes to fill them. Reports were conflicting as to the attitude of the various trade unions. In Alabama they seemed to be taking a normal course of integration, but unions in Arkansas, Louisiana, and Mississippi and in the Louisville, Kentucky area had taken no public steps to end discrimination. Negroes were often denied opportunities for training or apprenticeship, and then were not hired for lack of training or experience. Yet from Little Rock, Arkansas, and from Atlanta, Georgia, especially in the transit field, came reports of distinct progress. The worst discrimination, one Negro leader said, was against Negro women. "Men can usually find jobs as truck drivers or something but the Negro girl high school graduate is virtually barred from the positions most women normally enter," he said.

Turning to another human problem, it is only natural to ask what meaning can be attached to exhortations to domestic virtues, when a young married couple are told abruptly by real-estate agents that there is no hope of their escaping from the teeming racial ghetto, because their appearance in a given suburban neighborhood would so frighten landowners, actual or prospective, that property value would immediately be lowered.

Sermonizing over patience becomes a mere mockery, as long as such patience is not a preliminary to positive action. No amount of interior resignation will wipe out the social stigma of carrying an outward appearance different from that of the white majority. Negro citizens in my own home country of New England whose parents, or grandparents, taught in the town's public schools and whose ancestors fought in the Revolutionary War will still find career doors slammed in their faces today. Yet the same doors are flung nobly open for the escapee from a foreign country who has been but a couple of weeks in the United States. More power to the escapee, and to the generous American spirit that welcomes him! But the "offensive" Negro can but wryly join in the patriotic congratulations.

Hence a very difficult choice of attitudes today faces the young Negro.

If he is balanced and fairly philosophic, he will not be overly disturbed; he will not allow himself to be socially paralyzed by these hindrances, leftovers from slavery and postslavery days of the past. He will value good work done tirelessly to eradicate the evil: by legal action in the National Association for the Advancement of Colored People (NAACP), by social progress in the Urban League, and will work generously with the various religious agencies in the field. Yet at the same time he will be sorely tempted to despair. Race nationalist movements, such as the Black Muslim League, fantastically irrational in themselves, can serve as a powerful emotional outlet.

As Father Fichter points out, the American Negro had high hopes from the growth of industry, but the harsh reality of employment discrimination—or its correlative, the "last to be hired and first to be fired" principle—can make these hopes turn sour.

II

It is not my aim to add to the abundant data so authoritatively supplied by the other writers in this volume. I wish simply to emphasize one point that, in my experience, is peculiarly essential and decisive. The turn of the road which Negro youth may be expected to take at this present juncture—whether to confidence and renewed effort or to race fanaticism and blind despair or surrender to the wiles of Communist propaganda, will be determined to a considerable degree by the hope that the white majority places in the Negro himself: by the positive or the negative view that we take of Negro men and women as constructive components of our American civilization.

Does the young American Negro feel that he—or she—is essentially, by the very nature of things, just a problem to be solved? solved with all compassion and wisdom, solved by all the socially therapeutic skill which is at our command, yet essentially and predominantly a *problem*, something that we wish were "not there;" and we could act so much more freely if that "problem" were not around. Or does he feel that we are persuaded, intelligently convinced, that the presence in our midst of this minority group is, in its own mysterious way, a precious gift of the Creator to our nation? Are we *more* American, more truly ourselves, more genuinely a united and strong people, precisely *because* the Negro American is part and parcel of our history, of our national culture, of our highest moral ideal?

There are vital and far-reaching ways in which this query may be stated. We can propose it, for instance, from the standpoint of national security. In so formulating it, we may remember that in the Korean War it was the young Negro GI's who would not and could not be brainwashed by the Chinese Communists when, alas! so many of their heroic white comrades fell victim to that peculiarly diabolical assault. It is not enough today to be considerate of the Negro's needs and problems, and to strive to see that he shall get a square deal, important, essential as this is. A deeper philosophy is needed. The time has come for a profound evaluation of the Negro's dynamic contribution to our economy, to our national social structure, to our American culture, and particularly to the moral fiber of our civilization. At a time when there is much talk about "conservatism," it is essential to remember that the Negro is a genuinely conservative element in our nation: not by a blind adherence to past forms, but as one who has borne the heat and burden of our entire national history. His fate is specially tied up with the history of our nation. A hundred years ago the American Negro entrusted his lot to our nation's federal principle; and today our country, in the stress and strain of world pressures, faces the question whether or not it will remain faithful to the solemn pledges it made when a century ago it freed the Negro from slavery.

In a world where three-fourths of the human race are nonwhite people, we discover, to our bewildered surprise, that the Negro's presence here can be the source of unexpected strength at home and honor abroad. We have only just begun to gauge the future constructive function of Negro youth to President Kennedy's Peace Corps which, significantly enough, makes its debut in East Africa.

The Catholic Interracial Councils of the United States, over forty in number at the time of writing, have operated and continue to operate since their inception in June, 1934, on a simple but enormously fruitful principle. They hold that the diversity of racial groups in our country is not just a problem to be solved, but is the source of positive blessings, the opportunity to build a stronger nation. They are furthermore a living demonstration of the Church universal: not as an abstract and merely nominal attribute of catholicity, but as catholicity dynamically exemplified in every diocese or parish where the races have learned to work together. Or, to stress this point still further, there is no more creative form of community—whether it be the civic community or neighborhood, or the religious community of the Church—than one in which the various racial groups collaborate for the common good: the common good, that is to say, not set up as an abstract and merely social entity in order to absorb and diminish the dignity and responsibility of the individual, but in the true Thomistic sense, as an expression of the full personality of the individual, in all the dignity and responsibility with which he is endowed by the Creator.

A galaxy of inherited depreciatory customs, paternalistic attitudes, derogatory semantics, accepted myths and slogans has militated in the past against such a positive view of people of other race or color. Not least of these was the erroneous concept of race itself, which Father Gleason so effectively exposes; or, in the language of Father North, juristic projections such as the Plessy separate-but-equal doctrine, which took the place of educational reality. Such doctrines, as Dr. Anastasi explains, lead to pessimism and despair. Our country has no greater interior danger than a vast, articulate, mobile, despairing minority, linked by sentiment and origin to other despairing masses of the globe.

Some may say to me: you are laboring the obvious. Well, would that I were. My trust is that what is thus laboriously explained may prove overwhelmingly obvious a few years hence. Yet in fact, these truths are as yet by no means obvious to a large segment of influential public opinion. Some of our most widely diffused slick weeklies purporting to keep us up to date on world and national news, make it apparently a point uniformly to depict the racial situation in the most dismal light. Stories of the riots in some of our large cities, of the tragic events in the Congo, of the alleged difficulties of integration (ignoring its progress and the steady increase of successful achievement), revived stories of the Reconstruction days after the Civil War, crime narratives and the like can all go into the hopper of pessimism, and lend themselves readily to the purpose of the Communist monger of racial hatred abroad.

Such dismal predictions serve their purpose. They place a brake on silly optimism; they cause us to check our facts, and to remember that crime, ignorance, and degeneracy are always with us. Most of all, they remind us that in the field of race relations we cannot just happily drift. Unless we wish to yield the field to the extremists and let the forces of violence take over, it is time for us to adopt a positive and constructive philosophy, not only work together for a morally, religiously, culturally, and economically stronger America, for peace in our neighborhoods through interracial deliberation and cooperation, for patient study and thoughtful communication and deliberation, for dynamic group action in our parishes, and for a living exchange of spiritual life and experience, as well as for a widespread program of popular education in the interracial field. These are not matters we can postpone until next year or next month, but matters that press on us today. The time is now. And if we do not adopt this positive and cooperative attitude here and now, we are leaving the door open to the subversive forces—from outside and from within—that can rend our nation to pieces.

III

On May 1 of 1961, one of the most beautiful countries in the world, the Republic of Tanganyika in East Africa, embarked on its independent national existence, under the strong leadership of its gifted young Prime Minister, Julius Nyerere—strong, precisely because of his insistence that "freedom" can bring to a new nation life and vitality, not as a merely negative idea, but only as a positive concept, recognizing the full worth of every individual in the republic, whatever his racial or national origin, and guaranteed by constant and patient cooperation among all divergent elements in the republic.

Abraham Lincoln's Emancipation Proclamation of 1863 was not just a noble humanitarian gesture toward an oppressed race, restoring their civil rights, and thus recognizing their human rights as well. It was above all an act of faith in what the Negro people had to contribute to the Union. It was an act of faith in their future, and of hope that they would respond to the challenge of freedom.

President Lincoln had been sharply blamed for not following a very different course. Delegations sought to persuade the President to purchase all slaves, free them, and settle them. Yet he refused to see these delegations, or to interest himself in the charters of corporations which undertook to finance the shipment of freed slaves back to Africa and to parts of South America.

Abstracting from the quixotic unrealism of such a "repatriation" there remains the simple consideration. It was Lincoln's judgment that this country, not Africa, was now the home of the descendants of the first slaves, and that these descendants were wanted, not for some mere tactical reason, but as an integral part of the republic. They were, in other words, Americans, and toward the reborn nation had a mission to execute that no others could fulfill. Was this verdict on the positive worth of the Negro people (irrespective of the particular opportuneness then and there of the Proclamation) a mistaken judgment on Lincoln's part, or was it an act of inspired wisdom? On our answer to this question will depend in great part our attitude toward the intricate political and legal and social questions that the liberation of the Negroes has involved. Our choice of an affirmative or of a dilatory and hesitating answer to the highly crucial question of the desirability of the Negro as a citizen will condition in great measure our serious, solid, and consistent effort to value the Negro people as a source of strength and integrity for the Church.

It is easy, of course, to talk pastoral statistics and to reply that all souls regardless, and so forth, are equally precious in God's sight. And this is entirely true. But the Church, dealing here not with discarnate spirits but with the concrete circumstances of our existence, cannot ignore the earthly conditions under which men seek their salvation. The question, therefore, in the Negro's mind, is just how far does the Church understand these realities; how far will the Church aid the individual in coping with them; how far is the Church sincerely interested in the Negro's struggle for decent living conditions and a just share of the nation's welfare?

Collectively and singly, the Bishops of the United States have given in recent times a resoundingly affirmative answer to this question. Would that it had been given at an earlier date! Do the lay people of the American Catholic Church echo it? That is the problem which the organized Catholic interracial movement has set itself to solve, and seeks to mobilize the many resources of the Church to that effect. Nothing, however, is accomplished by mere shouting in the dark. Actual problems exist; they cannot be solved by facile formulae, still less by dramatically staged sudden "changes of heart." To an extraordinary degree, they are rooted in the changing metropolis and the struggle against the all-embracing ghetto, and are linked with all the great economic and cultural and social-action questions of our times. Laborious, humble, cooperative effort of majority and minority groups is needed, in organized and systematic fashion, coupled with—or resulting in—a wide program of popular education, such as is being now proposed by the 106,000 members of the Third Order of St. Francis through its 1,600 fraternities in the United States.

However far these inquiries may range, and complex as are the details, it remains true that the presence of the minority groups has added new depth, reality, and meaning to the Church's teaching on the Mystical Body; spiritual vitality for the American Church in its relation to the same Mystical Body throughout the world; new intensity and realism to the sublime doctrine of the Incarnation and its mysterious relation to the multiplicity and unity of the human race.

Hence the importance of the studies collected in this volume. They provide effective tools with which we can make real progress in our lifetime work of building the City of God.